CANOE TRAILS THROUGH QUETICO

D1527069

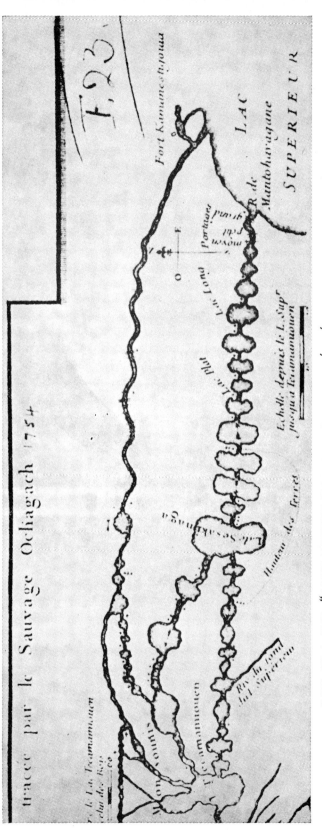

PART OF A MAP, "CARTE PHYSIQUE DES TERREINS LES PLUS ÉLEVÉS DE LA PARTIE OCCIDENTALE DU CANADA" ORIGINALLY PUBLISHED IN *Considérations géographiques et physiques sur les nouvelles découvertes* BY P. BUACHE (PARIS, 1753–4); THIS SECTION CAME FROM A ROUGH SKETCH OF THE COUNTRY FROM LAKE SUPERIOR TO LAKE OF THE WOODS WHICH AUCHAGAH (LA VÉRENDRYE'S SPELLING) DREW ON A PIECE OF BIRCHBARK IN 1728.

CANOE

TRAILS

THROUGH

QUETICO

By Keith Denis

DRAWINGS BY
SELWYN DEWDNEY

The Quetico Foundation

Distributed by
University of Toronto Press

Reprinted 1967, 1971, 1974, 1980

ISBN 0-8020-3046-7

Quetico Foundation Series

1. THE INDIANS OF QUETICO. By E. S. Coatsworth
2. QUETICO GEOLOGY. By V. B. Meen
3. CANOE TRAILS THROUGH QUETICO. By Keith Denis
4. INDIAN ROCK PAINTINGS OF THE GREAT LAKES. By S. Dewdney & K. E. Kidd
5. CANOE ROUTES OF THE VOYAGEURS. By E. W. Morse
6. QUETICO-SUPERIOR COUNTRY. By B. M. Litteljohn
7. WILDERNESS CANADA. Edited by Borden Spears
8. PLANTS OF QUETICO AND NORTHERN ONTARIO. By Shan Walshe

Foreword

BY BLAIR FRASER

FOR anyone who has ever travelled the canoe routes of Quetico Park, reading Keith Denis's book is an exercise in pure nostalgia. It brings back some of the happiest, healthiest days of his life, spent in what must surely be the finest canoe country in the world.

It is not easy to describe the peculiar charm of Quetico. The fishing is good but not sensational, the scenery delightful but not spectacular, the dozens of lakes not markedly different from each other or from many lakes on Canada's Precambrian Shield. What gives Quetico its special quality is a unique blend of past and present, history and geography. Here, preserved like a gilded fly in amber, is the Canadian wilderness as the explorers and fur traders knew it centuries ago, the Canada that caught the imagination of Samuel de Champlain and the Chevalier de la Salle, the Canada that David Thompson surveyed and Alexander Mackenzie travelled.

In the case of the two last-named, and of all the other great names of the fur trade, the statement is literally true—they did paddle through these very lakes, carry over these very portages. You can still travel, as six of us did a few years ago, over the old *voyageur* highway using the narratives of Mackenzie and Alexander Henry and the geographer Dr. John J. Bigsby as your guide to the portages and campsites.

In a way, of course, you can do that on other parts of the route that ran from Montreal to Lake Athabaska—but how different most of them look today. Towns and farms, power dams and factories dominate the scenery now, and the cry of the loon gives way to the roar of outboard motors and the jangle of juke boxes. To escape these things you must go many miles north of the settled parts of Canada, and even then you don't always succeed.

Except in Quetico! Here lie a million roadless, houseless

acres on each side of the international border—Quetico Park in Ontario, Superior National Forest in the United States— which are still ours to keep inviolate, the last accessible remnant of the cleansing wild.

I hope Keith Denis's book, the work of a man who was born in the Quetico country and knows it as few others do, will bring thousands more Canadians to know this delightful bit of our national heritage, and send them home again determined to protect it.

Acknowledgments

THE Quetico Foundation would like to acknowledge the courtesy of the Dominion Archivist, Dr. W. Kaye Lamb, in the matter of assistance in connection with the map which appears as a frontispiece. The Department of Lands and Forests* of the Province of Ontario has most kindly made available for our use in this book its map 56A, on which we were graciously given permission to superimpose suggested canoe routes through Quetico Park.

*Now Ministry of Natural Resources

Contents

FOREWORD, by Blair Fraser   v

ACKNOWLEDGMENTS   vii

Then and Now   3

The Outfit   9

Canoe Routes   16

Before the White Man Came   74

Bibliography   80

Remember!   82

Birds of Quetico   84

CANOE TRAILS THROUGH QUETICO

CANOEING INSTRUCTIONS IN 1650
QUETICO—SUPERIOR AREA

THE INSTRUCTIONS of Father Le Jeune to young missionaries on the handling of a canoe and behaviour *en route* are as applicable today as they were 300 years ago when the Jesuits were moving into the West from Quebec and Montreal.

"You should be prompt in embarking and disembarking. Do not carry either water or sand into the canoe. It is not wise to ask too many questions nor should you yield to the itch for making comments about the journey, a habit which may be cultivated to an excess. Silence is a safe and discreet plenishing. Should there be a need of criticism, let it be conducted modestly.

"In brief, it is well to be cheerful, or at any rate to appear so. Everyone at the portage should try to carry something according to his strength, be it only a kettle. For example do not begin paddling if you are not prepared to continue paddling. Stick to your place in the canoe. Be assured that if once you are set down as a trouble maker and difficult person, you will not easily get rid of such a reputation."

Then and Now

VOLCANIC FORCES built mountains of Precambrian rocks and subsequent earth-building epochs added many changes, but the characteristic topography of Quetico Provincial Park is largely the result of the advance and retreat of the great Keewatin and Labrador ice sheets. Gone with the glacial drift deposited in Minnesota and Iowa are the pre-glacial river valleys and all evidence of the mastodons, giant beaver and other pre-historic creatures that lived in the first forests. Indeed, the ice gouged down until only the stumps of the ancient mountains remain. So vigorous was the scouring that even today the striated surfaces of many ice-polished rocks indicate the direction in which the mile-deep ice sheets moved.

Later, warm winds blew across the earth; the glaciers retreated, leaving the moraines, eskers and kames common to the region. The present disarranged drainage system became established: a tangle of rivulets flow in every possible direction and the main streams occupy ice-gouged stress zones and old lake-basins. Eventually, the waters of the Quetico leave the park in the southwest corner, on their way to Hudson Bay.

The lakes show endless variety. Some are over twenty miles long; others are little more than ponds. Rock cliffs rise majestically from some waters; others are bordered by beaches of fine sand. Islands and peninsulas are common landmarks. Waterfalls and rapids are numerous on the streams that connect the lakes, but when the waters are not navigable, relatively short portages provide a way to bypass the barriers. Quetico Provincial Park is ideal canoe country.

Pierre Esprit Radisson and Sieur des Groseilliers may have been the first white men to enter the Quetico country. They spent the summer of 1660 going from "isle to isle" but Radisson's narrative is too vague for his travels to be traced with certainty.

In 1688 Jacques de Noyon wintered at Rainy Lake and

within five decades, La Vérendrye established the French outposts in the West. The lilies of France were replaced by the flag of England soon after the battle of the Plains of Abraham. Over the years restive Indians plundered traders and burned abandoned posts along the Grand Portage Route from Lake Superior to Lake of the Woods, but their dependence upon European goods enabled the Scottish and English traders who provided them to regain control of the waterways.

Furs were in great demand across the Atlantic, and rivalry for the trade was keen. The powerful North West Company found itself opposed in the Quetico area by the Hudson's Bay Company in 1793. Later the XY Company, formed by Alexander Mackenzie, and Jacob Astor's American Fur Company, had posts on border waters. Finally, in 1821, the North West Company merged with the Hudson's Bay Company. An agreement was made on March 21, 1833, with the American Fur Company, which withdrew from the Rainy Lake, Winnipeg and Red River districts for an annual payment of £300, leaving the Hudson's Bay Company in control of the waters about the present international boundary south to the height of land.

The international boundary between Canada and the United States, long disputed, was settled by the Webster-Ashburton Treaty of 1842. It provides that subjects of both countries may use the waterway and portages along the Grand Portage Route.

In 1857 an expedition sought an all-Canada route of travel between Lake Superior and the Red River Settlement. George Gladman was in charge, Henry Youle Hind was its geologist and naturalist. The surveyor on this expedition was Simon J. Dawson, and his name has been given to the route which was recommended. It leads through the heart of what is now Quetico Provincial Park. There was little activity along the Dawson Trail until 1870 when Sir Garnet Wolseley used it to bring troops from Canada to suppress the Métis uprising led by Riel in Manitoba. Soon after hundreds of immigrants passed over this route to the Canadian West. Oxen, horses and wagons were used on the portages, where wheel tracks can still be traced. Steam tugs and launches plied the lakes pulling barges laden with merchandise. It took six days to travel from Port Arthur to Fort Frances. After 1876, however, the railway from Duluth to Moorhead, Minnesota, and the Red River side-wheelers provided an easier means of communication and the Dawson Trail was seldom used. Then the Canadian Pacific Railway provided a direct route from eastern Canada to the prairies after 1885, and the Quetico waterways were abandoned.

Quetico Provincial Park was established in 1909, largely through the efforts of W. A. Preston, Member of Parliament for Rainy River District. It contains about 1,750 square miles of territory. The Ministry of Natural Resources of Ontario is making the Quetico a canoe country without peer. No private buildings may be erected within the park and aircraft can land only at a few designated spots on the perimeter.

The scars of early timbering operations are well covered and modern cutting regulations ensure that the scenery of the Park will not be spoiled. Hills green with their cover of aspen, birch, ash, spruce and pine surround a myriad sparkling clear lakes. Portages where the earth is still hard-packed by the moccasined feet of the *voyageurs* lead to realms of solitude. The trails of Indian, fur-trader and immigrant can be followed with an inner surge of adventure. Relaxation comes with the dip of the paddle, the flight of an osprey or in watching the leaping tongues of flame in the evening campfire while the loons call across the lake.

SPEED RECORDS IN QUETICO CANOE COUNTRY

David Thompson, famed explorer, trader and surveyor, in 1797 travelled from Bottle Portage to Grand Portage in five days, a surprising record. On the return journey, he left Grand Portage August 9th, reached Saganaga Lake on the 14th and arrived at Fort Frances August 20th, taking twelve days instead of the customary fifteen to seventeen days.

George Simpson, Governor-in-Chief of the Hudson's Bay Company, was noted for the swiftness of his movements over the waterways of Canada in the early 1800's. When he brought his wife west, he did not slacken his pace. Lady Simpson tells in her diary (1830) of starting, apparently at Twin Lakes, at 1:00 A.M., crossing Sturgeon Lake and entering Maligne River at 6:00 A.M. Lac La Croix was reached by noon and, despite torrents of rain, at 7:00 P.M. they camped on Rainy Lake, probably by Kettle Falls. The trip from Fort William to Fort Frances took from May 26th to noon on June 1st—just six and a half days!

These astonishing trips were made with picked crews of five to eight paddlers who were undoubtedly familiar with the route and directed by leaders who had the ability to obtain the full co-operation of their men. These records still stand.

PRESCRIPTION FOR ENJOYMENT

Getting the most out of a vacation is an ideal. In the sections of this book which follow are suggestions which it is hoped will help anyone who decides on a canoe trip in Quetico Park to achieve his objective.

One of the first requirements is a detailed map of Quetico Provincial Park, and with this book one is provided, on a scale of 2 miles to the inch. Topographic survey maps of the area, on a scale of 4 miles to the inch, are also available and extremely useful. Poring over maps and planning a trip is half the fun, as hundreds of people know who on winter nights have selected the route they will take through the Quetico. You'll need the map and the book on the trip, and a plastic envelope will protect both from rain, dirt and tearing.

Fishing may be the magnet that draws you to the sparkling waters of the Park. When you arrive with your rod and reel, you will find the Park Rangers and the local residents ready to tell you where the big ones wait and the lures to use. Don't bring minnows because by law you cannot use them. But you can find lakes that are seldom fished where you may be the first person to cast a line into the place where the big ones lurk.

Walleyes, usually called pickerel in northwestern Ontario,

6

are caught in many lakes throughout the Park. Northern pike and lake trout are also common, and small-mouthed bass occur in some lakes. Anglers must secure a special Provincial Park Licence from the Ontario Department of Lands and Forests to use their rods in Quetico waters. These are available at Park Headquarters at Nym Lake, at the French Lake Campsite, at ranger stations on La Croix, Basswood and Saganaga lakes and from outfitters. May, June, September and October are the best months for anglers.

The history of the region fascinates visitors and a knowledge of the past adds to the glamour of many a view. A later chapter of this book describes briefly the Indians the white men found. Even while the snow lies deep on the hills you can travel with the pioneer adventurers through the region by reading the tales of their travels. See the bibliography on page 80. *The Voyageur's Highway* by Dr. Grace Lee Nute, published by the Minnesota Historical Society in 1941, tells the story of the border-lakes region and it lists many books now out of print that may be in your local public library.

The trip itself will bring many enjoyments. Flowering plants brighten the woodland scene in constantly changing array from spring to fall and the fruits of blueberry and pin cherry provide a pleasant supplement to meals. Glimpses of wild life reward those who approach feeding grounds quietly, especially at dawn and dusk. The smaller birds are most noticeable in early summer when their territorial songs vibrate through the forests. Later there are scurrying flocks of waterfowl and soaring eagles to watch. To help the traveller recognize what he sees, a field guide is invaluable.

By means of photography the members of a canoe trip can see where they have travelled long after the last portage has been crossed. Rushing rapids, a tent among the towering pines, a glowing campfire: these are but a few of the subjects that can take the attention time and again on a Quetico vacation.

Perhaps most rewarding of all is the thorough relaxation that comes with solitude. Beautiful lakes away from the main canoe routes afford retreats where in a golden silence there is

RECUPERATION FROM THE CONSTANT TENSION OF MODERN LIVING

an opportunity to recuperate from the constant tension of modern living. Frayed nerves rebuild themselves away from the roar of machines and other blaring noises of modern civilization. Quiet days bring a new strength.

The Outfit

THE VOYAGEUR of the fur trade was a husky lad who carried two or three 90-pound packs at a time over portages. From dawn to dusk, he was expected to paddle at a six-mile per hour pace while he lived on grease and corn, or pemmican—a mixture of fat, dried buffalo and drier berries. Asleep or awake, he was the food supply for black flies and mosquitoes. Those who survived got used to it.

Today you, the holiday *voyageur*, usually have but two weeks a year to spend canoeing and it would be folly to endure the hardships the early travellers would so gladly have evaded. Keep your packs light. Give yourself a chance to get into condition—plan to travel short distances the first few days. Eat well, rest well and enjoy your visit to Quetico.

You may prefer to use the services of an outfitter instead of transporting everything required from your home. Should

GIVE YOURSELF A CHANCE TO GET INTO CONDITION

9

this be your plan, make your reservations well in advance to ensure that the equipment and supplies you need will be available on your arrival. Complete or partial outfitting service is provided. Competent guides can be secured through outfitters. A guide can lessen the amount of physical effort required on a trip and teach inexperienced adventurers how to meet the problems that can arise in the woods. For information about outfitters write to

> The Atikokan Chamber of Commerce, Atikokan, Ontario
> The Fort Frances Chamber of Commerce, Fort Frances,
> The Thunder Bay Chamber of Commerce, Thunder Bay,
>   Ontario*

or

> The Quetico Foundation, Toronto, Ontario.

THE CANOE

Aluminum canoes, 16 to 18 feet long, are the more popular craft today but many still prefer the canvas canoe for the

METAL CANOES WILL STAND A LITTLE MORE PUNISHMENT

10

*The cities of Port Arthur and Fort William amalgamated January 1, 1970, under the name Thunder Bay.

silence of its gliding motion. Metal canoes will stand a little more punishment from rocks and are usually lighter. Both types can be carried easily when provided with a properly adjusted yoke. Pick suitable paddles and take a spare one. Add a length of light rope (a 25-foot length of clothes line is good) for lining or tracking the canoe. Repair kits are a "must" for all types of canoe. Tested life jackets are good insurance.

You won't get far in the Quetico without a canoe so you must be careful how you treat it: ramming a canoe into rocks can easily damage it. Before starting, learn how to handle a canoe. Common sense among canoeists is imperative. Don't overload; pack heavy articles in the bottom of the craft and in such a way that they will not shift with the motion of the waves. Load slightly stern heavy. Do not travel when high winds blow or during thunderstorms. Do not run rapids unless you are an expert canoeman and then only after first inspecting them. Children should know enough to sit still—and they should not be frightened or startled, even in fun. Pull your canoe clear of water when on shore—you would feel very silly watching it drift away. In fewer words: "Don't tempt the Fool-Killer!"

THE PACK

The first essential is to provide yourself with good outdoor clothing and boots that will not fall apart if they get wet. Check the following lists, which suggest necessaries every pack should include.

Clothes
1 cotton shirt
1 woollen shirt
1 pair trousers
extra pants
1 pair boots
1 pair running shoes
2 pairs light wool socks
1 windbreaker jacket or slicker
   or raincoat

1 hat or cap
1 bathing suit
sweater
neckerchief or bandana
pajamas

Toilet articles
towel
soap
shaving kit

brush and comb
First-aid kit (including nail file)
needle and thread
sunburn cream
aspirin
toothbrush and paste
5 handkerchiefs (or kleenex)

Personal items
flashlight and new batteries
4 plumber's candles
bug bomb
fly dope

compass
fishing tackle and rod
pocket knife
camera and film

Optional
sun-glasses
ball of twine
tobacco and pipe
mouth organ
field-glasses
notebook and pencil
plastic bags
playing cards; etc.

FOOD

Rubbing two sticks together will produce fire, but it takes time. Make certain you have plenty of *matches*, and pack some of them in a *waterproof container*. You will be astounded at the number of matches used when smoking "makings" or a pipe.

A 2½ lb. single-bit *axe* with a 26-inch handle is almost standard equipment. If you are the type that chops granite boulders (and who isn't?) bring along a *file* and *whetstone*. Add a *folding saw* to your kit and your firewood problems will be greatly simplified.

Fireplace *grates* are a luxury but make cooking much easier. After you find yourself with a green pole burnt in two and your fire drowned with soup, you will likely tie one of these to your packsack. A reflector *oven* is another useful luxury. Driving rain presents another problem for cooks that can be licked by tucking a tin of canned heat in your pack. Inside the tent, you can heat water for soup or beverage over the tiny flame. Remember, a small wood fire cooks the meal and uses less fuel, while a big fire results in both food and cook being half-baked if not slightly burnt!

Nested mess outfits for two, four or more persons with all necessary cooking and eating utensils are easy to pack. Canvas carrying bags for the nested outfits keep other packsack contents cleaner. The cook will need:

2 pots with covers	1 can opener
1 frying pan	1 large mixing spoon
1 sharp butcher knife	1 wide steel spatula

And make certain everyone has a *knife, fork, spoon* and unbreakable *cup* and *plate. Soap that floats,* a *Chore Boy* and a *dish towel* have their place too.

Dehydrated foods lighten the packs and provide a wide choice of tasty dishes. Many are pre-cooked and these save time when the chef is under fire from hungry voyageurs. A word of warning: read the instructions before starting on the trip—sometimes something more than water has to be added. The recipes on the boxes should be followed if you want compliments on your cooking ability.

There is a can and bottle ban. Take some plastic bags to hold partly emptied packages of boxed foods.

Food check list (two persons; 12 days; about 70 pounds)

Coffee—8 oz. instant	Soup mix—6 packages
Milk—1 lb. Milko	Onions—6 medium
—1 lb. cream	Bovril—2 cubes
substitute	Steak—1 lb. (for first night)
Tea—30 2-cup bags	Sausage—1 lb. (for first break-
Cocoa—½ lb.	fast)
Sugar—6 lbs.	Meat—enough dehydrated
Syrup—2 lbs. heavy	meats for 7 meals
Jam—24 oz. tin	Bacon—5 lbs. (in piece)
Apricots— 1 lb. dried	Eggs—2 doz. fresh or
Prunes—1 lb. sugaripe	dehydrated
Raisins—1 lb. seedless	Cheese—2 lbs. cheddar
Puddings—2 pack. instant	Butter—3 lbs.
Cookies—2 lbs.	Shortening—1 lb.
Pepper—1 shaker	Potato—2 4 oz. package in-
Salt—1 lb.	stant
Chocolate—2 bars semi-sweet	Rice—2 lb. package instant

Beans—1 lb. pack. pre-cooked	Pancake mix—2 lbs.
Spaghetti—1 package with	Rolled oats—1 lb.
sauce	Bisquick—1 package
Bread—3 loaves	Spanish Rice—1 package

The above list has been tested in use and provides enough food for a 12-day period if you plan to eat freshly caught fish as the main course at 6 meals. While planning your trip, prepare a complete menu for each meal you will eat on your trip. This will give you an excellent check on the quantity needed. Substitute your favourite foods for those listed but don't cut down on quantity. You will be surprised at your appetite.

Enjoy your catch! Fish should be killed, drawn and dried immediately after they are caught, especially during rainy weather. Bacteria develop rapidly on a moist surface and gastric juices can eat into the flesh, causing a taint. While drawing, remove the gills and scrape the kidney from along the backbone. Hanging fish up in the shade where a breeze will dry them for a few minutes will aid in keeping them wholesome. Fish should not touch each other while being carried or they will soften. Dry grass or moss is excellent in the creel as it allows the air to circulate. A good rule is to catch only enough fish for the next meal.

SLEEP

A wall-style silk *tent* with a mosquito bar is ideal. The manufacturer will provide a suitable bag for carrying it. Pegs and poles can be cut in the wilderness if you fail to find them on arrival at any of the many campsites awaiting you in the Quetico. It is seldom necessary to cut a tree and good woodsmen never hack them down too close to the campsite. Terylene or down-filled *sleeping bags* with removable liners and zippers so they will open completely for airing are recommended. *Air mattresses* provide needed comfort, and don't forget the repair kit. A lightweight *tarp* 6′ × 8′ is a handy addition to the outfit: it can be used as a floor in the tent or to cover your packs if you are caught in the rain or as an emergency shelter.

Some mushrooms and berries are edible, others are not; it is as well to leave them alone unless you are positive they are not poisonous. Be careful with your axe. Standing up in a canoe is as reckless as diving deep into unknown waters. Avoid sunburn. Be sure you can recognize poison ivy.

Above all, be careful with fire. Build your campfire on soil or rock, make it a small fire, and when you leave, be certain it is out. Drown it. Stir the ashes to make sure no spark remains. If you smoke, remember, one careless action can destroy the beauty of the region.

BE CAREFUL WITH YOUR AXE

WILDERNESS MANNERS

Keep the campsites clean. Burn paper, trash and garbage. Pack out tins, bottle caps, glass and other unburnable refuse in plastic bags. When you clean your fish, burn the parts you discard. Clean campsites will not attract multitudes of flies, wasps and other insects, or bears. Don't cut or scar trees unnecessarily. Don't deface Indian rock paintings or lichencovered cliffs. Don't move or steal historic relics along the route.

Canoe Routes

IN the following pages 15 canoe routes will be described, 1–9 in detail, 10–15 in outline. The network of waterways through Quetico Provincial Park provides opportunities to alter the routes outlined simply by following other waters than those listed. Maps should be used. Portages should be accepted as challenges. Travel times given below are average but do not allow for time which may be lost owing to high winds, rain, fishing or relaxing. Double the times given—and double your enjoyment.

Many canoe routes can be navigated safely by novices, and in fact, only the upper stretches of the Kawnipi River, the Basswood River and the Quetico River (including the Namakan River to Lac La Croix) require any considerable amount of experience.

Families will undoubtedly enjoy the trips where campsites are frequent and the waters easy to paddle. Experience shows that families prefer lakes to rivers, and tend to avoid rivers like the upper Kawnipi and the Quetico. However, when an experienced canoeist or guide is along, there are no difficulties which cannot be surmounted on any route described below.

PUBLIC PARKS AND CAMP GROUNDS

French Lake: Ranger cabin, auto park, tent sites, Park museum, nature trails, dock and picnic ground. Airport.

Nym Lake: Park Headquarters. Airport.

Nominal fees are charged for some of the services provided.

CANOE ROUTE NO. 1: THE DAWSON TRAIL

AREA: French Lake to Lac La Croix
TIME: 6 days, round trip
DISTANCE: 48 miles of paddling; 1¼ miles of portages

The stretch from French Lake to the start of the Maligne River and back again is easy for beginners. On the stretch from the start of the Maligne River to Lac La Croix, the downstream journey is easy but the steady upstream pull on the way back might be discouraging to inexperienced paddlers. The current below Tanner Lake requires strong paddling for a couple of hundred yards.

The Dawson Trail is a historic route. Part of it lies outside the Park and part within.

The Dominion of Canada was created July 1, 1867, and three years later it took over the administration of Rupert's Land from the Hudson's Bay Company. Mistakes in policy for the West resulted in the election of a provisional government at Red River, now part of the Province of Manitoba. Louis Riel soon became the leader of the Council of Rupert's Land but annexationists, Fenians, land-hungry newcomers and rowdies who despised the half-breed inhabitants caused disorders. To establish control of the area, the young Dominion sent west a military expedition of 1,431 men under the command of Lieutenant Colonel Garnet Wolseley. The transportation of this field force from Prince Arthur's Landing on Thunder Bay to Fort Garry, now Winnipeg, was the responsibility of Simon J. Dawson.

A forty-five mile road was built from the present Port Arthur to Shebandowan Lake, where the troops embarked on July 16, 1870, in boats which had been battered when being hauled up the Kaministiquia River from Fort William. The weight of the boats varied somewhat, those of the clinker construction being from 650 to 750 lbs. and of the carvel, from 850 to 950 lbs. The expedition moved forward in brigades of six boats. Each boat, with its crew of eight to nine soldiers and two or three Indians or half-breed *voyageurs*, was a self-contained unit. Sixty days' provisions were carried—salt pork, preserved vegetables, flour, biscuits, tea and sugar. In addition, the load included trenching tools, ammunition, tents, waterproof sheets, blankets, cooking utensils, boat-builder's tools, white lead, mosquito oil and other essentials. Certainly not a load that would make portages welcome!

17

The route from Shebandowan to French Lake covers a distance of 76 miles by water and 4½ miles by land. Shebandowan Lake, where the troops embarked, is long and narrow. The Indian name of the lake means "wigwam with both ends open" and a medicine lodge of the Midewiwin—the Grand Medicine Society of the local Ojibwa Indians—is believed to have stood on the shores. The lake is now a popular summer resort and lake trout, walleyes, northern pike and small-mouthed black

SIXTY DAYS PROVISIONS WERE CARRIED. IN ADDITION . . .

bass are caught in its waters. Deer and moose leave tracks along the shores and ruffed grouse are often seen along the trails.

Twenty-one miles west of the landing is Kashabowie River, a turbulent stream necessitating a portage of three-quarters of a mile. Today, Highway 120 crosses this portage. Wolseley's boats had to be dragged over this and other portages. Small trees were felled across the path to act as rollers and forty to fifty men would haul on a tow rope.

Kashabowie Lake was a ten-mile row to the mile-long Height of Land Portage that leads over a hill to Lac des Milles Lacs. Between islands, the course continues to Birch Narrows and on to Baril Portage where the Dawson Trail joins the Kaministiquia Route. Now came a 350-yard portage, eight miles across

Baril Lake to the quarter-mile Brule Portage, and then the
fifteen-mile stretch of Lake Windigoostigwan: this is a route
still in use. The two-mile French Portage to French Lake is
overgrown but can still be followed. However, it is as unpopular
as ever and Highway 120 which crosses it provides an easier
though longer portage.

THE DAWSON TRAIL WITHIN QUETICO PARK

French Lake is today the embarkation point for many trips
through the Quetico. An eloquent Indian chief, nicknamed
"Blackstone" because he argued so well for the rights of his
tribe, had his encampment at French Lake in 1872. Captain
Huyshe mentioned seeing a humming-bird here in 1870, the
first record of this species in the Park.

1¾ MILES*. *French Lake.* Starting from the sand beach beside
the dock, skirt the big wooded island in this lake which
is almost in direct line with the reedy entrance of the
winding channel to Pickerel Lake.

1¼ MILES. *Pickerel River* is a smooth-running stream. In season,
blooms of blue iris, orange lilies and yellow swamp candles
brighten the banks. Near the mouth, you glide over the
remains of an old dam.

11 MILES. *Pickerel Lake.* On entering the lake, sand beaches
are to be seen on the southern shore. The Point of Pines,
on the left past a great jutting spit, is a one-mile paddle.
Here the Department of Lands and Forests maintains a
fine campsite where you can pitch your tent under towering red pines whose needles litter the ground. Great blue
herons frequent the slough at the end of the sandy beach.
Along the rocky northern shore, pickerel are caught.

From here to the first portage, you travel westward across
the lake. The rocky point of Lookout Island is the first
target; then turn southward and round Emerald Island
where campsites can be found. Now paddle to the south
shore of the Lake and follow it into a deep bay leading to
Pine Portage. Below the surface of the water near the
beach rest the remains of an engine, believed to have

*Approximate distance between points

19

belonged to a steamer which plied the waters of Pickerel Lake between 1870 and 1878.

594 YARDS. *Pine Portage* is well cleared, and fairly level. The first seeds of the red and white clover found along the way probably arrived with hay for the teams of oxen that hauled wagons loaded with the luggage of immigrants on their way to the fertile prairies. The hard-packed tracks of the creaking wheels remain as evidence of their passing. A Hudson's Bay Company post stood here about 1857. Henry Youle Hind called this the "Portage des Morts" and said this name arose from the painful death of a *voyageur* who was crushed when he lost his footing while carrying a heavy North canoe. A few heaps of cobble stones mark graves at the east end of the portage.

1½ MILES. *Doré Lake* is crossed to the southwest bay where an old barge is sunk just beneath the clear waters. The rocky landing is just beyond. Chestnut-sided warblers nest nearby.

704 YARDS. *Deux Rivières Portage* is a long, hard trek, but the brush is well cleared and a rest at the top of each rise gives you time to catch your breath. Smear on a little flydope before you start. Go over the first rocky slope; down into a swamp where a corduroy road keeps you out of the muck some of the time; over another steep hill and down into a valley; cross a small stream on a log runway; climb up again and then plunge downhill to the landing.

¾ MILE. *Twin Lakes*, not named on the map, are separated by a shallow. In dry weather, you will have to walk on the hard, rocky bottom and to pull your canoe through. Here, on June 9, 1843, John Henry Lefroy, on his way to search for the magnetic north pole, wrote sentimental verses on a sheet of birch bark.

1¼ MILES. The *stream* out of the Twin Lakes is weedy and meandering. The early travellers called it Grass or Hay River. The map shows three portages but these are merely pull-throughs. The southernmost is the remains of an old lumber dam which has been breached. The Delaware Portage once bypassed this stream, and it was on that road that Patrick O'Leary in 1875 met "Blackstone" whose uniform was a red coat of the George IV period, cavalry pants and cocked hat.

The stream enters Sturgeon Lake through a prolific growth of reeds. On the return trip the entrance can be found by watching for the break in the tree line.

16 MILES. *Sturgeon Lake* is a series of sand bars at first, where reeds rustle against the sides of the canoe. The Pickerel River enters on the east. After passing south through a narrow channel, the lake widens. On your right is an island with a good campsite. On the small island a mile south is another camp ground and from here the ranger cabin on the eastern shore can be seen. The view from the Lookout Tower on the western heights is worth the climb. Then on, through Sturgeon Narrows, by the islands, to a long sand spit on the east shore that is the finest camp ground in the park. Five miles on is the entrance to the Maligne. A sunken barge and a boiler lie in the waters of Sturgeon Lake near the first landing.

The *Maligne* (or *Bad*) *River* presents three beautiful rapids in quick succession. The portages are all on the western bank of the stream. Large trees along the trails show cable scars made by winching logging boats over the old wagon roads.

242 YARDS. First portage: marshy landings are at both ends of this level and wide portage.

¼ MILE. Go along the wide river with its many families of mergansers to a rocky ledge.

352 YARDS. Second portage: remnants of the old corduroy road, bits of logging chain and blueberries the size of small marbles make this an enchanting spot to camp.

1 MILE. Now an easy paddle along the river to another rocky landing.

220 YARDS. Third portage: another blueberry portage, easy to cross if you are blind to the tempting fruit. Downstream is a good campsite.

2¼ MILES. Flat Rapids is easily run.

1½ MILES. The river widens.

3½ MILES. *Tanner Lake* is named after John Tanner, who was captured by Indians when 11 years old and adopted into a tribe with whom he lived for thirty years. In 1823, he was persuaded to return east and to put his daughters in a school. He told his wife, a native of the country, of his plans to leave her. The result was that an Indian relative shot and left him wounded on this island. Fortunately for him, a fur brigade picked him up and took him to Dr. John McLaughlin, of Oregon fame, at Lac La Pluie post.

25 YARDS. At the west end of Tanner Lake, there is a short portage on the south side of May Island. It goes over a small island and is rocky all the way. There are good landings. Here is another campsite.

4¼ MILES. Downstream on Maligne River the going is good until opposite the lower end of May Island. Here is a great eddy and it is followed by another. On down past an old logging company landing on the right bank just upstream from Trail Creek. A mile further on is a flat rapids. Another mile, and on the left bank is the junction with the route to Minn Lake. Here the rocks have weathered to an unusual wart-like appearance. Downstream, on the north side of the south channel around Lou Isle is a landing above Twin Falls.

60 YARDS. Photographers will enjoy the opportunities at *Island*

BELOW SNAKE FALLS TENTS CAN BE PITCHED

22

Portage. An old Dawson dam can be seen on the south side but the fall on the north side of the island is a stretch of foaming white water.

2¼ MILES. The open waters of *Lac La Croix* are entered [2¼ miles] by passing Beil Island lying to the south. The Dawson Trail now leaves Quetico Park.

Along the northern shore is the Neguaguon Lake Indian Reserve with a village at the mouth of the Namakan River. The alternate route back from Lac La Croix is by the rapid and turbulent Namakan River to Namakan Lake. Below Snake Falls and above High Falls, tents can be pitched. Fish the eddy below High Falls if you go this way.

THE DAWSON TRAIL BEYOND ISLAND PORTAGE TO FORT FRANCES

Lac La Croix	21 miles
Beatty Portage	286 yards
Loon Lake	4 miles
Loon River	4 miles
(3 short portages)	
Little Vermilion Lake	6 miles
Sand Point Lake	9 miles
Namakan Lake	16 miles
Kettle Falls Portage	short
Rainy Lake	44 miles

This represents a total of 104 miles by water and half a mile by land. A four-mile portage from the western end of Lac La Croix to Sand Point Lake eliminated the Loon and Vermilion Lake section after 1870 but this became overgrown when the Dawson route was abandoned. Today, the Campbell truck road uses part of the old trail.

Fort Frances, an outfitting point for Quetico-bound parties, was headquarters for the Athabasca fur brigades in the centuries before lumbering made it an important paper manufacturing centre. Before the abandonment of the Dawson Trail, $200,000 was spent on locks that were to allow steamers to bypass the falls and travel 116 miles down Rainy River and across Lake of the Woods to North-West Angle Bay where a 95-mile road had been built to Fort Garry. Wolseley's expedition found the road unfinished and followed the English River trail to Fort Garry, which they reached August 24, 1870, just 55 days after leaving Thunder Bay on Lake Superior. Later the journey from Prince Arthur's Landing to Fort Frances took about six days.

The Dawson Trail was used for about twelve years. A military force of 215 men with two artillery pieces passed over it in October, 1872, and in the following year, also in October, the first three divisions of the North-West Mounted Police crossed over it. W. H. Carpenter and Co., of Orillia, secured a contract to operate the line to Red River in 1874. They advertised "Prince Arthur's Landing to Fort Garry, Emigrants $10.00, children, half fare. 200 lbs. personal baggage free; extra baggage $2.50 a hundred. Emigrants should take their own provisions." The route was never popular even after tugs and barges were used on the larger lakes. The railroad from the east to St. Paul offered a faster and more comfortable trip and the advance of the shining rails across the Dominion doomed the Dawson Trail as a route for immigrants. However, it served its purpose by providing a route west when needed. Today, the signs of the past add to the pleasure of a canoe trip through this unique wilderness.

CANOE ROUTE NO. 2: THE GRAND PORTAGE ROUTE

AREA: Saganaga Lake to Lac La Croix
TIME: 7 days, one way
DISTANCE: 67 miles of paddling; 2¾ miles of portages

From Saganaga Lake to Lac La Croix the going is easy for beginners; the return journey is upstream—but with ordinary caution on Basswood River there should be no difficulties.

Beaver and birch made this the highroad of the fur-traders for seventy-three years. The bark of the white birch was built into canoes, light to carry over portages yet sturdy enough to bear a fortune in beaver pelts. The Montreal canoe or *canot du maître* used on the Great Lakes was about forty feet long while the *canot du nord*, fifteen feet shorter, was used inland. Surprising loads were carried in these unique craft. David Thompson, in describing Grand Portage about 1797, wrote: "The Merchandise for the winter trade of the distant trading Posts

24

was here assorted, and made up in pieces each weighing ninety pounds; the Canoes were of a less size, and the load was twenty-five pieces; besides the provisions for the voyage and the baggage of the Men: being a weight of about 2,900 pounds, to which add five Men, the weight a canoe carries will be 3,700 pounds."

Coureurs de bois knew of the route long before it became the *voyageur*'s highway but they did not advertise their illegal trade. Pierre Gaultier, Sieur de la Vérendrye, opened this pathway to the west in 1731 when he sent his nephew, La Jemeraye, to build Fort St. Pierre on Lac La Pluie. Brigades of trading canoes followed and the woods re-echoed to "A la claire fontaine" and other songs as the paddlers sped across the lakes.

New France abandoned the posts in the "upper country" in 1759 and Indian uprisings made travelling dangerous until 1771. The mysterious "Franceway" (François Le Blanc) crossed the Quetico portages on his way to Red River in 1765 and venturesome men like the audacious Thomas Corry and intrepid James Finlay followed him. John Askin had a fort built at Grand Portage in 1768 and traffic westward increased until in 1774 more than sixty canoes went inland.

Competition resulted in corruption of the Indians, arguments between adventurers, business failures and killings. To counteract these troubles, the more reputable traders began to co-operate and soon business agreements united the traders.

The North West Company was first organized in 1779 and the names of the traders sound like a roll call of the Clans of Scotland. Simon McTavish, William McKay, Archibald Mc-Leod, William McGillivray and other Highlanders made Grand Portage the great inland depot of the fur trade. "Pedlars" they were called by the rival Hudson's Bay Company factors, for they brought goods to the Indians instead of waiting for the Indians to come to the posts. The trade expanded and reached the Pacific Ocean and the Arctic Circle. In 1803, to avoid threatened difficulties with American customs officers, the North West Company moved to Kaministiquia and fallen trees soon blocked the Grand Portage Route.

"This is the Headquarters or General Rendezvous for all who trade in this part of the world" wrote Daniel Harmon of the Grand Portage of 1800. The North West Company fort, twenty-four by thirty rods, stood about twenty paces from the shore of a shallow bay on a gentle slope. The base of 703-foot Mount Josephine touched the northwest corner. Cedar pali-

"PEDLARS" THEY WERE CALLED

sades, about eighteen inches in diameter, sunk three feet in the ground and rising about fifteen feet above, surrounded the space. The roofs were of pine and cedar shingles and the doors, window frames and posts were painted Spanish brown. Six buildings were storehouses for furs and merchandise; others were dwellings for the bourgeois and clerks, a counting house, a large mess hall and blacksmith and other shops. At night the gates were shut and two sentries posted to keep watch, mainly for fear of fire. Two hundred rods to the east, the XY Company had a smaller post.

Grand Portage was a quiet place eleven months of the year. But early in July, the partners of the enterprise would begin to gather at the post. Furs from the north and provisions and merchandise from the east would change hands, the share-holders or their representatives would hold their business meeting and the canoemen would relax before preparing for their return trips. About one thousand men would crowd the area. The North men would live under tents while the "pork-eaters" from the east would sleep under their canoes.

"At this period," wrote Alexander Mackenzie, "it is necessary to select from among the pork-eaters, a number of men, among whom are the winterers, sufficient to man the North canoes necessary to carry, to the river of the rainy lake, the goods and provisions requisite for the Athabasca country; as the people of that country (owing to the shortness of the season and length of the road, can come no further), are equipped there, and exchange ladings with the people of whom we are speaking, and both return from whence they came. This voyage is performed in the course of a month, and they are allowed proportionable wages for their services."

The portage which gave the route its name was a hard trek. The *voyageurs* divided the eight and one-half miles into sixteen poses or resting places. Alexander Henry, on July 19, 1800, walked over it to Fort Charlotte in two hours to write: "The portage was very bad in some places, being knee deep in mud and clay, and so slippery as to make walking tedious." *Voyageurs* were expected to carry eight pieces across; usually two at a time under their contract. For each additional piece carried, they received from six livres Grand Portage currency to one Spanish dollar.

Today, Highway 61 bisects the old portage trail and connects at Mineral Centre with a road to Lake Superior where the fort has been rebuilt and houses a museum. The portage has been cleared to the site of Fort Charlotte on the Pigeon River. The water route beyond is largely unchanged, a challenging wilderness.

ROUTE TO THE BORDER OF QUETICO PARK

Fort Charlotte was evidently an old post in 1793 when John Macdonell, a newly engaged clerk at the time, wrote that "Mr. Donald Ross has been so long in charge of Fort Charlotte that he has acquired the respectable name of Governor." Today, rectangular mounds overgrown with grass indicate where the buildings stood. Two miles upstream 69-foot Partridge Falls necessitates portaging 440 yards on the American side and a rocky shelf provides a good campsite.

The "Prairie," three miles up the shallow stream, was the customary stopping place for the *voyageurs* the first night above Grand Portage. Here "All were merry over their favourite regale, which is always given on their departure, and generally enjoyed at this spot, where we have a delightful meadow to pitch our tents, and plenty of elbow room for the men's antics." No other campsite is found until Fowl Portage is reached. How the *voyageurs* felt the morning after we can only imagine but they could have felt little enthusiasm for the day ahead. Half the load had to be carried for miles along the stream while their companions, waist deep in water at times, worked the canoes up among the rocks and rapids. A mile and a half above the "prairie" was a 485-yard portage on the right bank, known as the Great Stone or Grosse Roche portage. A third of a mile above was 540-yard Caribou portage. The river then becomes better for canoeing and three miles up, on the Canadian shore, is the 2002-yard Fowl Portage.

Fowl Lake aroused the enthusiasm of Dr. John Bigsby, the artist-physician, who was assistant secretary of the British-American Boundary Commission: "We enter it by a long portage, woody like the rest of the environs, and overlooked at its west end by a basaltic precipice not less than 600 feet high. The view from the summit is beautiful. A strong north-east gale was blowing across a clear sky successive companies of clouds, which mapped the sea of woods before us with fugitive shadows. Looking to the north-west, Lake Outard lay below, nearly bisected by a rushy narrow. Beyond it we have hilly ranges of woods, running W. N. W., with long narrow valleys between. To the south and south-east we see the valley of Pigeon River buried in dark pines, among which we still discern short silvery traces of the stream itself. . . . Lord Selkirk attempted to form an agricultural establishment on the low lands about this lake; but it failed, and is deserted." The French "Outarde," translated, is "bustard," the name the English traders gave the Canada goose. Later the two parts of the lake were called Hen and Cock lakes.

South Fowl Lake can be reached today by a private road to the eastern shore. A 4-mile paddle and North Fowl Lake is left by a 750-yard carry over Moose Portage. Four miles long, Moose Lake was the "Original" of the French, and the "Elk" lake of Mackenzie who declared "Here is an excellent fishery for whitefish, which are exquisite." The Hudson's Bay Company and the American Fur Co. each built a post here about 1824.

Great Cherry Portage, 800 long yards over a hill, leads to quarter-mile Vaseux Lake. Vaseux, sometimes called Little Muddy or Second Cherry, Portage is 300 yards in a dry season. Fan Lake, another lily pond like Vaseux, is crossed to the 250-yard Lesser Cherry Portage at the end of which is a campsite. A 6½-mile paddle past the picturesque shores of Mountain Lake brings one to Watup Portage, 500 yards over hills and gullies on the American bank to Watup Lake, a narrow line of water between high hills. Two miles or so down this lake is the "Petit Detroit," a narrow shoal that often forces a stepover portage. The mile of water from here to Long Portage is called Rove Lake on American maps. The swampy 1½-mile Long Portage leads to Rose Lake.

Lake trout attract anglers to the campsites on Rose Lake. The middle of the lake is very shallow over ooze but there is deeper water along the southern shore. Indians gather wild rice from the marshes in season. On the north, a stream joins Arrow Lake. High mountains rise above the green slopes about Rose Lake and the narrow upper portion ends at Rat (formerly Marten) portage. Twenty paces across a rocky ridge is Rat Lake, a mud pond with abundance of white waterlilies. Then 300-yard South Lake Portage leads to South Lake, 1551 feet above sea level, 949 feet above Lake Superior. Two and a half miles west is Height of Land Portage and a campsite where the *voyageurs* generally finished their small kegs of spirits. The proprietors of the fur trade used good psychology in providing a supply of liquor for the men when the arduous Pigeon River headwaters were reached. The thoughts of the revel to come probably kept the men from rebelling against the swift pace upstream. Once over the 500-yard Height of Land Portage, the currents would favour the *voyageurs* for hundreds of miles.

Voyageurs who crossed this portage were entitled to wear coloured feathers in their caps for they were no longer "pork-eaters" of the east but had been baptized "Nor'westers." Each novice was sprinkled with a cedar bough dipped in water. Among the initiation promises was one not to kiss a *voyageur's* wife without her consent! The ceremony ended with the new "Nor'wester" buying drinks for all present.

Another custom, long evident on the waterways that led through the Quetico country, was to make a lob pine or "Mai" on a prominent point by cutting all the upper branches from a tree except for a tuft at the top. Usually this was done in

A CAMPSITE WHERE THE VOYAGEURS GENERALLY FINISHED THEIR SMALL KEGS OF SPIRITS

honour of a bourgeois or distinguished traveller who was then expected to provide a round of High Wine.

North Lake saw the end of a dream about the turn of the century. An ambitious project to link Port Arthur by rail with Duluth ended on the Canadian shore where the abandoned roadbed of the Port Arthur, Duluth and Western Railway can still be seen. Long abbreviated to P. D. & W., the line once was nicknamed the "Poverty, Distress and Want."

The course is first north and then west through Little North Lake, for 2¾ miles in all to a 55-yard portage. Here, on the American side, is a marine railroad with a manually operated capstan. The traders called this "Décharge des Epingles"; a "décharge" being the spot where the canoe must be unloaded wholly or in part and then let down stream by a rope while the portion of the cargo removed is carried overland.

Little Gunflint Lake narrows within a mile and a half and then widens into the seven-mile stretch of Gunflint lake. Resorts, reached by the Gunflint Trail from Grand Marais, 41 miles south, lie on the American shore. The railbed of the Gunflint and Lake Superior Railway can still be discerned. The Pigeon River Lumber Company Limited obtained charters from both the Canadian and the United States governments and built this logging railroad in 1902 to connect with the P. D. & W. at North Lake. It operated for about eight years. When the white pine was gone, the rails rusted.

At the northwest corner a strait 8 yards wide leads to Magnetic Lake and 1¼ miles on is a rapid followed by a 12-foot falls that drops over three steps of rock. From Lake Superior to this point the canoe has been paddled 60 miles and carried for 15 miles.

Starting at the portage round this falls, the columnar listing provides a comparison of maps and names.

Distance	*Sheet 52B*	*Headed upstream, portage on:*	*U.S. Chart 808*	*Fur trade names*
50 yards	(unnamed) P.	Right	Little Rock P.	Ladder or L'Escalier
1 mile	Pine River		Pine River	
380 paces	Blueberry P.	Left	Wooden Horse P.	Le Cheval du Bois
⅓ mile	Pine River		Pine River	
556 yards	(not shown)	Left	Granite River P.	Portage des Gros Pins
1⅜ miles	Pine Lake			
50 yards	P. (unnamed)	Right	Granite Lake P.	little fausille (sickle)
¼ mile	Granite Lake		Granite Lake	
⅓ mile	Granite River			
181 yards	(not shown)	Left	Swamp Portage	Descharge du vaseu
¾ mile			Granite Bay	
143 yards	(not shown)	Left	Granite River P.	"the cedars"
⅓ mile			rapids	"the Chats"
¾ mile	Granite River			
88 yards	P. (unnamed)	Left	Gneiss Lake P.	Stone rapids
¾ mile	Round Lake		Gneiss Lake	
1 mile	Devil's Elbow L.		Devil's Elbow L.	
176 yards	(not shown)	Right	Maraboeuf Lake P.	Marabow, Maraboeuf
			U.S. Chart 809	
1¼ miles	Maraboeuf Lake		Maraboeuf Lake	Maraboeuf Lake
99 yards	Horsetail Rapids	Right	Horsetail Rapids	descharge
⅜ mile				
33 yards	Saganaga Falls	Left	7′ Saganaga Falls	2nd Petite Rocher de Saganaga

This entails 8½ miles paddling and 10 portages totalling 1,626 yards. Campsites will be found at Wooden Horse Portage, Granite River Portage, Granite Lake and on Saganaga Lake. The U.S. charts are easier to follow.

Saganaga Lake is on the southeast edge of Quetico Park. Alternate routes to this beautiful lake of islands are: (1) Drive from Thunder Bay, Ontario, over the Silver Mountain Road to Whitefish Lake and on to Arrow Lake which connects with Rose Lake. (2) Leave Highway 61 at Hovland and drive to McFarland Lake. (3) Motor from Grand Marais, Minnesota, 54 miles up the Gunflight Trail to Sea Gull Lake. These first three routes connect with waters leading to Saganaga Lake. A highway between adjoining Northern Light Lake and the Atikokan Highway is in the planning stage.

"There was formerly a large village of Chipeways here, now destroyed by the Nadowessies (Sioux). I found only three lodges filled with poor, dirty and almost naked inhabitants, of whom I bought fish and wild rice." This was Alexander Henry's description on July 20, 1775.

Cache Point, on the northern shore of Saganaga Lake, is near a seaplane base and Ontario Ministry of Natural Resources Ranger station. The first portage is 2½ miles southwest, past the narrows.

22 YARDS.* *Swamp Portage,* a level portage on the Canadian side ends on a muddy walkway.

½ MILE. *Swamp Lake.*

418 YARDS. *Monument Portage,* three bronze boundary markers give this portage its present name. The eastern part of this clear and well-marked portage is in poor condition as the log runway through the swamp needs repair. There are steep grades at the middle and western end.

5¼ MILES. *Cypress Lake*—the fur-traders' cypress is our cedar. This lake is also known as Otter Track. Glacial striae on the columnar greenstone bear southwest, showing the direction the glaciers moved across the area.

*Approximate distances

66 YARDS. *Little Knife Portage*, clear and level, on the American side, was once known as Petite Rocher des Couteaux.

3 MILES; 7½ MILES. *Little Knife Lake* connects by a narrow channel with *Knife Lake*. Fish for walleyes in these clear waters. A blue-black, flint-like rock that breaks with sharp edges is said to give the lake its name. It occurs locally on the mountainous shores.

506 YARDS. *Big Knife Portage* on the Canadian side, leads around a rapids to Knife River. The ruins of a lumber company dam and log chute lie across the head of the rapids. Between the excellent rocky landings is a wide trail, with Knife Lake slate covering ancient corduroy. This portage is now about 400 yards in length according to some estimates. The Swallow-Hopkins Lumber Company cut the forests on the American shores from Knife Lake to the Pictured Rocks on Crooked Lake.

¼ MILE. A short quarter-mile paddle downstream leads to a rapids.

22 YARDS. Portage to Seed Lake is on left going downstream. A continuation of this portage for another 100 yards leads to quiet waters and is used going upstream. Dr. John Bigsby rhapsodized about the size and variety of water lilies which are found in almost every lake. This, and the other Knife River Portages, can be shortened by pulling through the shallow rapids when conditions are suitable.

¼ MILE. *Seed Lake*.

132 YARDS. Portage on United States shore should be used during spring floods or in dry years. A shorter but rough portage can be made across a small island at the head of the little falls—22 yards or less—to a shallow and rocky riffle.

⅓ MILE. *Knife River* and *Melon Lake*.

88 YARDS. Portage, on American side, is in fine condition. The rapids can be run in periods of high water.

1 MILE. *Carp Lake*, once called Pseudo-Messer Lake. The land around was fire-swept prior to 1916 when Arthur L. Parsons of the Geological Survey, Canada, visited the area. Today, the scars are well hidden. Excellent campsites are located near the portages.

264 YARDS. *Carp Portage.* Well marked and fairly level, on the American side, with good landings on beaches at both ends with a campsite.

4¾ MILES. *Birch Lake* and through a channel into Sucker Lake. A 75-yard portage can save a 2-mile paddle if one plans to head through Newfound and Moose Lakes to visit Ely.

110 YARDS. *Prairie Portage* is clear but has steep grades. David Thompson saw a burnt house on the old portage on August 16, 1797. Indians nearby demanded 60 beaver skins for a new canoe. A dam at the head of the rapids has changed

DR. JOHN BIGSBY RHAPSODIZED ABOUT THE WATER LILIES

the course of the river but it is believed Indians camped on the Canadian shore for many years. In 1910, fire swept from the American shore along the portage. The western end of the trail passes between the Canadian Customs house and the ranger station.

17 MILES. *Basswood Lake*, Z-shaped, was called Lac Bois Blanc by Alexander Mackenzie, who added "but I think improperly so called, as the natives name it the Lake Pascau Menac or Dry Berries." The Rev. J. A. Gilfillan gave the

Ojibwa name as "Bassemenani" and translates this as "Dried Blueberry Lake." The first syllable may have suggested the present name.

The French had an outpost here, and later the North West Company built a wintering house. Later still, in 1824, Simon McGillivray represented the Hudson's Bay Company here. The trade must have been of some considerable consequence because Thomas McMurray, a Chief Trader, wintered on Basswood from 1825 to 1830. In 1831, an interpreter was in charge of the trade the year round. One early post was on the north side of a narrows between

EXPERIENCED CANOEMEN CAN SHOOT THESE RAPIDS

Bayley and Inlet Bay. In 1853, the Hudson's Bay Post was on Ottawa Island. Indians supplied the traders with wild rice, lake trout, northern pike and walleyes as well as furs and canoes. They likely used some of the canoe routes popular today.

Bayley Bay on the north shore is the gateway to the Agnes Lake Route. North Bay provides entry to the Kahshahpiwi chain.

On the southwest end of Basswood Lake is the Quetico-

Superior Wilderness Research Centre where forestry and other wilderness management problems are being scientifically studied. Close by, Hoist Bay connects by Long Portage with the route from Ely.

1,870 YARDS. Portage around *Upper Basswood Falls*, sketched by Bigsby in 1823 to illustrate his book *The Shoe and Canoe*. The good rocky landing is a few hundred feet above the falls on the American shore. Near by is a good camp ground. The trail around the 9-foot falls is clear and level except for several hundred feet of swamp. The *voyageurs* would have called this a 3-pose portage for their custom was to dogtrot a third of a mile and then rest. Similarly, when on the lakes they took a ten-minute break each hour and enjoyed a smoke; thus Basswood Lake became known as a "4 pipes lake."

This portage can be shortened by entering the river 396 yards below the start, paddling a short stretch of fast water and portaging again. Expert canoeists familiar with the river can run the rapids but the wisest course is to take the 1¼-mile trail the traders called Horse Portage.

½ MILE. *Basswood River*.

132 YARDS. The next portage, known to the French as Portage des Grands Pins (*Great Pines*), is on the Canadian side and goes over a hill. Experienced canoemen can shoot these rapids; and going east they are a wet pull upstream.

1½ MILES. *Basswood River*.

66 YARDS. *Wheelbarrow Portage* is on the Canadian side. It is well marked, clear with a steep grade on the western end. Approach this dangerous falls carefully, keeping to the right shore away from the small chute. Go round the fair-sized island in the middle of the stream past the dangerous waters, then past the entrance to the main section of the 12-foot falls and go west to the small bay where the portage sign will be seen. This portage has been lengthened by 200 yards so parties coming upstream will not have fast paddling through the rapids.

1 MILE. *Basswood River*.

75 YARDS. Portage around *Lower Basswood Falls*, formerly Portage la Croche, begins just upstream from a large rock

at the top of the falls on the Canadian side. It is well marked, clear and fairly level. A new 176-yard portage leads to a deep landing. There are good campsites on the American shore. A fine campsite three-quarters of a mile down Crooked Lake on the Canadian side is only half a mile from the Painted Rocks on the opposite shore.

The red paint used by the Indian artists has preserved this record of their passing. Here too, is Mackenzie's "Rock of Arrows" where Sioux and Ojibwa were both believed to have shot arrows into the cracks of the cliffs in defiance of one another.

18 MILES. *Crooked Lake* has currents up to three miles per hour in the narrows but these are easily navigated. There is a drop of about twelve feet from the east to the west end of the lake. Follow your map across these waters. Many of the bays lead to portages connecting with other lakes worth visiting. Table Rock camp ground, on the south shore four miles down the lake, is but one of numerous campsites.

638 YARDS. *Curtain Falls Portage* on the American side is a steep decline. One hundred and sixty years ago, Thompson noted that "many flocks of wild Pigeons fly past" and Passenger Pigeons were then a welcome addition to the cuisine. The two pigeons killed August 19, 1797, did little to reduce their numbers but shooting thousands for the market exterminated the species. Distasteful modern additions on this portage have destroyed the wilderness atmosphere locally. The older portage, 150 yards shorter, ends at the foot of the falls.

4 MILES. *Iron Lake* has camp grounds on the islands and walleyes in the water. Rebecca Falls, 23 feet high, is on the north side on the Namakan River and a trip over the portage trail provides a view of this beautiful fall. The old fur-trade route bypasses the river route and continues to Bottle Lake which is entered by a short liftover.

440 YARDS. *Bottle or Flacon Portage* is a difficult 400-pace jaunt. Three lakes where small-mouthed bass can be caught are not far distant.

26 MILES. *Lac La Croix* provides good fishing. The Indian

name was Nequawkaun Lake—"piece of wood put incision in maple tree"—and in autumn the occasional maples add a bright scarlet flash of colour to the sombre woods.

There is a question as to the source of the name of this lake. Some authorities credited the shape of the lake. An old cross that stood on the island just west of the 92°, 15′ meridian line has also been mentioned. L'Abbé Prud-'homme, in his "Pierre Gaultier de Varennes, sieur de La Vérendrye," relates the most credible tale. Sieur de la Croix accompanied Jacques de Noyon on his expedition of 1688 to Rainy Lake. Returning, La Croix was caught in a storm on the lake west of Isle des Chasseurs (Hunters' Island). The canoe upset. Two companions clung to the birchbark craft but La Croix was drowned. From this sad circumstance, the lake received its name.

The Pictured Rocks are about three miles up the lake on the cliffs of Irving (or Shortiss) Island. "The traveller has left his mark on this rock in various ways, some by name, some by date, and some by strange divice," wrote Major Delafield in 1823.

Two miles further, around the northwest corner of the island, is a campsite by the ranger cabin. Indeed good campgrounds are plentiful among the islands.

286 YARDS. *Beatty Portage*: The marine railway here is a narrow gauged track and there is a flat car to carry one out of Quetico Park waters.

OUTSIDE QUETICO PARK

5½ MILES. *Loon Lake*, a narrow watercourse once called Un-de-go-sa or Man-eaters Lake.

412 YARDS. There is another *Marine Railroad* here on the former *Mud Portage*.

5 MILES. *Loon River*, where the shores were fire-swept in 1917 and 1925.

3¾ MILES. *Little Vermillion Lake*.

2½ MILES. *Little Vermillion Narrows* which were formed by granite walls.

1 MILE. Canadian Customs just north of the entrance to Portage Bay.

7 MILES. *Sand Point Lake* to Namakan Narrows.

16 MILES. *Namakan Lake* has many wooded islands. Then *Kettle Falls* and a portage around the control dam built in 1914.

3 MILES. A narrow and rocky defile with a fair current leads to Rainy Lake.

39 MILES. *Rainy Lake* is the translation of the old French name, Lac La Pluie. The first map of this country called the lake "Tecamamiouen," a Monsoni word for the mist that rose from the falls on Rainy River. The shores of this lake are still rock but slope more gently than those along most of the "Old Route." Major Delafield said, "In the valleys I have seen several places where I could drive a tent pin!"

2 MILES. *Rainy River* to *Fort Frances*. La Jemeraye in 1731 built Fort St. Pierre on Pither's Point, two miles upstream from the falls and just above one of the two rapids on this part of the river. The North West Company built their fort half a mile downstream about 1787, and it was an important post, especially for the Athabasca traders, until 1821 when the Hudson's Bay Company made York Factory the main depot of the fur trade. It continued to be called Lac La Pluie post until 1830. The Governor-in-Chief of the Hudson's Bay Company, George Simpson, brought his young bride, Frances, here on his way west in the summer of that year. In honour of her visit, on September 25th, Chief Factor John Dugald Cameron, to the cheers of those assembled and the firing of guns in her honour, renamed the post Fort Frances.

CANOE ROUTE NO. 3: THE BACK TRAIL

AREA: French Lake; Kawnipi Lake; Saganaga Lake
TIME: 7 days, one way
DISTANCE: 70 miles of paddling; 2⅘ miles of portages

Caution on Russell River and stretches of river above Canyon Falls is suggested. Parties should have some experience of paddling upstream or an experienced sternsman. On the return trip, caution is essential just above Canyon Falls.

This route was used by the Indians long before traders entered the Quetico area. The first map of the region west of Lake Superior was drawn for La Vérendrye by an Indian named Auchagah (see Frontispiece). Fortunately, the great explorer forwarded the work of this untaught cartographer to his superiors in Quebec. Surprisingly accurate, it excels many later maps and indicates all the main routes to the west. The St. Louis River, the Kaministiquia, the Grand Portage and the Dawson Trail routes are all shown, as well as this waterway.

An old map of the Quetico area has the section of this route from Sturgeon Lake to Saganaga labelled "The Back Trail" and the label suggests it was used as a means of returning. Certainly it would have saved time between Saganaga Lake and Sturgeon Lake, as a look at the alternative canoe routes will prove.

The Back Trail is of unusual historic interest. This route might have been along the boundary waters. The Treaty of Ghent, 1783, defined the border as the "customary waterway" between "Long Lake" and Lake of the Woods. Long Lake doesn't exist and the location of the international boundary line was a matter in dispute for years. In 1823, commissioners chosen by both countries were in the field. The Americans said the Kaministiquia Route was the customary one while the British suggested the St. Louis River route. Major Joseph

THE LOCATION OF THE INTERNATIONAL BOUNDARY LINE WAS A MATTER IN DISPUTE FOR YEARS

Delafield, the American agent, travelled over the Grand Portage Route. The Indians at Saganaga Lake told him the lake discharged through a series of rivers and lakes into Sturgeon Lake. Here was a direct water route and Delafield noted that it would leave the lakes along the "Old Route," west as far as Lac La Croix, to the south of the line. Fortunately, no one could call it the "customary" waterway and finally the so-called "Old" or Grand Portage Route became the compromise settlement by the Webster-Ashburton Treaty of 1842.

1¾ MILES.* *French Lake,* the embarkation point, provides good fishing for walleyes. The weedy exit is in line with the big island from the French Lake Campsite Headquarters.

1¼ MILES. *Pickerel Strait,* the winding channel now entered, passes banks where red pines, birch and poplar shade the waters.

8¼ MILES. *Pickerel Lake* has also been called Lake Kaogassikok and Lake Dorade; these English, Indian and French names all refer to the walleyed pike, which is also called yellow pickerel and, correctly, yellow pikeperch. The fishing attracts hundreds of visitors and several sand beaches provide good campsites, the best being at Pine Point, a mile down the lake. Paddling for 5½ miles along the south shore, over some good waters for northern pike, one reaches the channel leading towards the first portage. After passing two small islands, a look at the Quetico Provincial Park map shows an island resembling a bird in flight. The east channel appears to be a short route to the portage but where this channel turns west, the shallows are cluttered with reeds, dead trees and boulders. Rounding the other side of the island, there is deep water all the way to the old Dawson dam which was rebuilt in 1956.

396 YARDS. *Bisk Lake Portage* begins at the west end of the dam at a rocky landing where the water is deep enough to bring the canoe in sideways. The trail is clear and fairly level, with one mud hole about 10 feet long. Blueberries and twinflowers, a familiar sight at many portages

*Approximate distance between points

throughout the park, grow here beside the rapids. The loading point is from water-washed boulders.

¾ MILE. *Bisk Lake*, after a short stretch of fast water, is crossed along the western shore to the river channel and on to where orange paint on the rocks marks the portage.

150 YARDS. The rocky portage to Beg Lake is on the south shore and is a short carry past a pretty falls. An antique survey post held by a mound of stones can be seen near the top of the falls.

1 MILE. *Beg Lake* has a narrows along which steeplebush flowers in August. The eastern shore is followed to the end of the lake.

10 YARDS. The portage to Bud Lake is just a step over flat rocks to a shallow rocky landing. In dry weather, this might be 22 yards.

THE PORTAGE TO BUD LAKE IS JUST A STEP OVER FLAT ROCKS

1¾ MILES. After paddling down a river stretch, *Bud Lake* is crossed by passing several islands to a rocky point. The landing at a rock ledge is behind a granite islet. Here is a fair campsite on flat rocks.

200 YARDS. The Portage to Fern Lake is marked with a sign and an old blaze on a large Norway Pine. White water rushes in spectacular fashion over a rocky decline. At the foot of the downhill portage a glance upstream is

rewarding. A large cedar stands on an islet surrounded by foaming white water.

1½ MILES. After a short stretch of fast water with one shoal, *Fern Lake* is reached. This is a shallow lake where fresh-water clams abound. Several dead Norway pines stand out among the live ones.

396 YARDS. The next portage is poorly marked. From a muddy landing on the right side of the river channel the trail passes over two fairly steep hills. The final breakneck descent to the river ends at a mud and rock landing. The rapids are a fine combination of boiling dark water and white spray.

¼ MILE. A stretch of river which widens into a large pond and then narrows is covered quickly.

374 YARDS. There is deep water to the landing ledge of rock at the next portage which is well marked on the right shore. No room to camp here but the rock is an excellent place to have a refreshing cup of tea before tackling the trail, which is almost a duplicate of the last. Brown lichens on the rock, cheeky chipmunks and darting kingfishers enliven the restful scene.

1½ MILES. Over the hump and launched again, the canoeist will find the river widens for a third of a mile, then narrows to a rapids which can be run easily by passing down the centre of the opening at the right. A long, reedy stretch of shallow water follows before the open waters of *Lake Olifaunt* are reached. On the north shore at the first long point is a fine campsite with a well-built log-and-pole table and a great stone-slab fireplace. Westwards, a mile or so across Olifaunt Lake, is an excellent 440-yard portage over a hill to Sturgeon Lake. This is the customary route but we prefer the river route for its beauty.

1 MILE. Paddle along the north shore. The entrance to the river is barred by the first rapids.

154 YARDS. Portage No. 1 is on the right bank, not marked, and the trail, while not well cleared, is not difficult. The canoe must be loaded from a high bank.

66 YARDS. A few hundred yards downstream is another shallow

rapids. Portage No. 2 is through the woods on the left bank and it takes a little manoeuvering to get the canoe into the water by the leaning cedar. Unmarked and not cleared recently, this still is not a hard portage to cross. If fortunate, you may see a hatch of glistening dragonflies and hear the red-eyed vireos.

¾ MILE. Down *Pickerel River* to another rapids, unmarked on the map.

66 YARDS. Portage No. 3 is a good carry over an island where pin cherries add a splash of colour in late summer. This rapids can also be passed by lifting the canoe over several ledges of rock on the right side.

5½ MILES. Pickerel River again, now a wide, reedy stream and into *Sturgeon Lake* and on through bur-reed, pond-weed and cattails until near the first narrows. After paddling through this channel, the main upper lake is reached. There is a good campsite on the south shore of the island west of the gap. Another island a mile south is also a good place to pitch a tent. Pickerel abound in these waters. The ranger cabin can be seen on the east shore of Sturgeon Lake, opposite the Fire Tower which crowns the summit of a mountainous slope. The steel tower overlooks many miles of the Quetico. *Sturgeon Narrows* widen soon after they are entered and here the waters of Saganaga flow into Sturgeon Lake. Look for a turkey vulture perching on any of the dead stubs on the west bank.

⅓ MILE. The river out of Russell Lake enters on the left, a fast-running stream, and strenuous paddling is required to gain the head of the rapids. The best course is on the right side, with care to avoid a flat rock under water at the top of the rapids. These rapids may be run downstream. An island just above the rapids is a good camp ground though wood must be gathered on the shores of Russell Lake. Winged visitors will make their appearance: herring gulls, spotted sandpipers, song sparrows and, at dusk, nighthawks. The pickerel fishing is excellent and northern pike are also caught.

3 MILES. Paddle across *Russell Lake* and see Chatterton Falls and the Grand Rapids where over 500 great logs lie jammed. During the highwater period of the spring "break-up" of 1942, a foreman of the J. A. Mathieu Lumber Co. Ltd. made the error of putting too many logs through the falls at one time and the resulting jam could not be cleared. An excellent campsite with a wildflower garden is to be found on the island opposite the falls.

418 YARDS. The portage to Chatterton Lake is around the point south of the falls. Bald eagles nest near here. The portage is poorly marked but is well cleared. From the rocky landing a steep hill must be climbed and then descended to a muddy edge. The field daisies growing at the top of the rise were probably seeded from hay used in the lumber camps.

2 MILES. *Chatterton Lake* is long, narrow and shallow.

396 YARDS. The Portage to Keats Lake is well marked; it is in the eddy of Split Rock Falls, an eleven-foot chute of white water. The far end of this portage is difficult as great boulders have to be used as stepping stones. The landing here is rocky and shallow.

1½ MILES. *Keats Lake* produces pickerel and pike. A good camp-site is near the narrows on the north shore. Another, with table and benches, is close by the white terraces of Snake Falls. A portage here leads to some extremely fast water where a line from shore may be needed to make the final fifty feet. Another 330-yard portage, rocky and rough, on the left bank then has to be faced.

286 YARDS. This Portage to Shelley Lake is easily missed.

1½ MILES. *Shelley Lake* is a series of swift currents with long bays leading in many directions. Moose and deer may be seen along the shallow bays where white and golden water lilies grow. Campsites are scarce until near the first portage. The island is a good camp ground where the roar of the rapids lulls one to sleep. This rapids can be run downstream, if you are careful to avoid the water-covered flat rock halfway down on the then right bank but otherwise keep to the right-hand channel. Look the rapids over before tackling it and if you are uncertain, portage.

22 YARDS. Portage across the island.

1 MILE. Shelley Lake is narrow here and it is easy to see where the Arctic three-toed woodpeckers have scaled patches of bark from some of the trees so that at first glance they appear blazed.

22 YARDS. Another short and easy island portage.

1 MILE. Shelley Lake and the channel from Kawnipi Lake meet near a good campsite on a hill rising from the south shore. The orchids growing here should be admired, but not picked, so that visitors who follow can enjoy them also.

2 MILES. Kawnipi channel is divided by islands and there are occasional swift currents but none are troublesome.

13 MILES. *Kawnipi Lake* is long and when the wind blows strong the best course is along the western shore in the shelter of Kasie and Rosie islands. Evidence of the great forest fires of 1936 is to be seen in the even growth of the pines in this section. All appear to be about the same age. Good campsites are available on both the small islands below Rosie island. South two miles, a route from Agnes Lake (5c) enters Kawnipi. By paddling along the bottom of Rosie and then southeast two miles, a big bay is reached which gives entrance to Murdoch Lake and the West Channel of Agnes River (Route 5b).

Across Kawnipi Lake is the opening to the long stretch of McKenzie Bay. An island campsite overlooks excellent waters for walleye. Five miles up, a narrow channel necessitates a liftover or a pull through the fast water. Two miles further on is the 880-yard portage to McKenzie Lake. Rumour reports Indian pictographs on a rocky cliff in this lake but their location is unknown. Perhaps you can find them and advise the Quetico Foundation accordingly.

Excellent camp grounds are found on the islands and

shores at the mouth of McVicar Bay. At one, an old forge recalls the days of lumbering operations. South two miles, the Agnes Lake East Channel Route (5 a) enters McVicar Bay and the camp grounds are well kept by the hundreds of Boy Scouts who paddle this waterway each year. Sometimes at night, while sitting around a camp fire, the sight of the mysterious Northern Lights will recall an old Indian belief that the shifting lights of the Aurora are the headdresses of dead Ojibwa warriors dancing in the Happy Hunting Ground.

Kawa Bay, five miles deep, is on the east shore opposite McVicar Bay. Tales are told of an old Indian encampment and painted rocks and a canoe route to Shebandowan Lake by the Wawiag River. Little is known about this and many other sections of the Park. Old maps call Kawnipi "Kahnipiminanikok" and "Knofiminanikok." Indian words both, but what is their meaning? Is it really "High Bush Cranberry Lake"? Anglers enjoy these waters for the sport provided by lake trout, walleye and northern pike. Did you know that the bones in the head of the pike are said to represent every weapon used by the Indians?

The south end of Kawnipi Lake is a narrow channel at Kennebas Falls, a pretty rapids.

50 YARDS. *Kennebas Portage*, on the west bank, from a shallow landing goes over a rise to a rocky shelf. A fair campsite on the hillside can be used.

¾ MILE. *Kenny Lake* has an excellent campsite on the north shore.

50 YARDS. *Canyon Falls Portage* is the roughest on the route. The landing is between two rocks at the foot of the falls and can be reached only by paddling straight up the swift current to the portage sign. The upturned rock formation makes the carry difficult. The churning white water in the canyon roars down a thirty foot drop. (When coming down stream, keep to the left bank away from the brink of the falls on the right.)

⅛ MILE. A short paddle to a ten foot falls.

47

440 YARDS. An uphill portage, a short paddle to *Koko Falls* and another 150 yard portage are eliminated by this new portage.

150 YARDS. Another portage (one map says 110 yards, another 198 yards).

THE LANDING CAN BE REACHED ONLY BY PADDLING STRAIGHT UP THE SWIFT CURRENT TO THE PORTAGE SIGN

¼ MILE. Paddle to *Little Falls*, an eight foot drop.

175 YARDS. Portage on left side over a good trail to a rocky landing. Just above here, a fairly strong current over a shallow requires a few strong strokes of the paddles.

2 MILES. *Wet Lake*, where raspberries grow abundantly by an abandoned clearing on the south shore. As you pass eastward through the narrows a blueberry point, on the south side, is worth a visit.

66 YARDS. Portage over a rock shelf on the north shore by a twelve-foot falls.

¼ MILE. Paddle across a widening of the river.

88 YARDS. A portage on the south shore is almost hidden in a little cove. Muddy at the start, it improves rapidly and ends at a rock shelf above the nine-foot falls.

¼ MILE. A stretch of river this length seems too short after several portages. Here some fast water demands steady and energetic paddling.

220 YARDS. The portage on the south shore, from one rock shelf to another, bypasses an eight-foot falls. Here is a campsite. Above are several currents over shallows. The 25-yard portage over bare rock is dangerous in high water periods.

12 MILES. *Saganagons Lake,* and it is 2 miles to a 286-yard carry across a long peninsula that shortens the trip by 6½ miles. The all-water passage is easier in hot, calm weather. The voyageur is now 99 feet above Lake Kawnipi. At the entrance to Saganagons Lake, the course meanders among the islands. A good campsite lies on the north shore.

616 YARDS. Portage uphill past Silver Falls, a 23-foot spectacle. Good fishing here.

3 MILES. *Saganaga Lake* and here the trip over the Back Trail ends at Cache Bay Ranger Cabin, which is also a seaplane base.

The return trip is downhill and downstream. Caution should govern the approach to the falls and rapids. Some parties, pressed for time, arrange to be met four miles from Cache Point at Sea Gull Lake where the Gunflint Trail Highway from Grand Marais, Minnesota, provides access to the edge of the Quetico.

CANOE ROUTE NO. 4: JEAN LAKE ROUTE

AREA: Nym Lake to Jean Lake and return
TIME: 7 days, round trip
DISTANCE: 61 miles of paddling; 3 miles of portages

This is an easy route for beginners.

Here is the trail for the ardent angler! Fine catches of pike, pickerel and lake trout have been taken in these waters. Here, too, are long lakes where canoes can glide by a landscape of infinite variety.

The new Quetico Park Headquarters are at Nym Lake and here is a good place to start on this trip. A landing with a dock has been provided near the parking lot and campsite.

2 MILES. *Nym Lake;* head for the southwest bay.

600 YARDS. A hilly portage, east of the old portage, has sandy approaches and a couple of muddy spots along the way.

(The former crossing is northwest a short distance. From a muddy start, a 396-yard portage leads uphill to a small pond. The last 50 yards include a very steep downhill stretch. The second portage, 154 yards over a hill is in poor condition and the landing is poor.) The new trail is to be preferred.

7½ MILES. *Batchewaung Lake* is crossed to the deep bay on the west shore. A campsite is passed on the point of the bay and another at the second narrows. Past a third point, the course is westward for 3¾ miles to a small river. A campsite is just above the lake shore on this stream.

1,320 YARDS. The well-cut portage starts by the creek and is on the west side all the way, downhill except at the very beginning.

3¼ MILES. *McAlpine Lake* has a campsite near the portage. The lake soon becomes a swamp with stumps in the water and many water lilies.

22 YARDS. Portage on south shore at end of lake.

¾ MILE. The river is clear of debris and when the water is high, the rapids disappear.

6 MILES. *Kasakakwog Lake* has campsites among the ramparts of granite on the north shore.

418 YARDS. A good portage on the left leads around a frothing rapids.

20 MILES. *Quetico Lake* is an easy paddle downstream from the foot of the rapids. The long V-shaped lake is narrow, seldom a mile wide. Young jackpine is covering the scars of a great fire. High cliffs rise from the water along the west shore. Campsites are scarce; a point on the east shore opposite Eden Island and another on the north shore just past the last large island in the eastward channel are good locations. The route finally turns south into a bay where a small island provides a good campsite.

66 YARDS. The excellent portage is on the west side of a stream flowing into Quetico Lake. A timber boom lies across the entrance to the rivulet and the dam and log chute with its baffle are in ruins; the narrow gorge must have been a headache for the river drivers.

¼ MILE. *Conk Lake* should be crossed to a tiny bay on the south shore.

164 YARDS. This unmarked uphill portage is hard to find. It is in good condition. An alternative is to find the entrance of the narrow stream and paddle up, over the remains of a beaver dam, then through a gorge where the water runs fast and into 11-mile long *Jean Lake*, noted for its lake trout and pickerel. The total distance to this point is 40 miles by water and 2,376 yards across portages.

THE NARROW GORGE MUST HAVE BEEN A HEADACHE FOR THE RIVER DRIVERS

THE RETURN TRIP

164 YARDS. Leave *Jean Lake* by portage, or creek.

¼ MILE. Cross *Conk Lake*.

66 YARDS. Portage.

2½ MILES. Over *Quetico Lake*. Turn east at the entrance to the bay and paddle to the end of the lake.

176 YARDS. A portage on the south side of a stream leads to a rocky landing. For the preservation of the canoe, it is necessary to walk in the water when embarking here.

Nearby the remains of an old log dam recall lumbering operations in the park.

¼ MILE. The slow-flowing stream leads through the remains of two beaver dams to a good landing.

110 YARDS. The rocky, uphill portage passes an old dam and log chute which have now collapsed.

2 MILES. *Lake Oriana* is divided by a strait into two sections and the route passes through the lesser and least interesting part of the lake, from one shallow landing to another. Anglers might find the upper lake rewarding.

748 YARDS. *Cedar Portage*, on the north bank, starts over low ground and is a rough trail ending at a muddy landing.

¼ MILE. The shallow flow of water peters out among stones just below a narrow fall.

20 YARDS. Portage over the ledge to a flat rock that provides an excellent place to lunch.

4 MILES. *Lake Jesse*, a long narrow lake, has two campsites on opposite points about halfway up the lake—the best on this route. The southerly section of Lake Jesse was alive with birds in July, 1957 when the writer was in the area. A rough-legged hawk wheeled in the sky above a great blue heron and two young which flew to a reedy inlet just beyond white water lilies. Two broad-winged hawks soared over the dark pines. Olive-sided and alder flycatchers performed aerial acrobatics while chasing flies and young Canada jays seemed everywhere among the tree branches. A sora fed on the muddy bank and flickers hammered on the dead aspen. A melody of song rose from the Labrador tea and alders as thrushes, warblers and sparrows boasted about their families.

880 YARDS. The stony, shallow beach fronts the mossy relics of an old lumber camp. Both red and white clovers are plentiful along the old wagon road. The corduroy trail is good and wide but swampy in two places.

⅓ MILE. *Maria Lake* is quickly crossed to a boulder landing.

330 YARDS. The portage is over the usual hill and down to a muddy start.

3½ MILES. *Pickerel Lake* and Batchewaung Bay connect by a

narrow strait. A good campsite in a hayfield by the old cabin site just below Pickerel Narrows can be used. This was the site of a Holmes and McCafferty logging camp. Another is on an island half a mile northwest of the strait.

3½ MILES. At the narrows leading towards *Batchewaung Lake*, the waters of Quetico Park are left behind.

950 YARDS. The truck portage is crossed.

2 MILES. *Nym Lake* is crossed to the campsite. The return trip entails a total of 20 miles of paddling and 2,860 yards of portaging.

Endless variations may be made in travelling to Jean Lake. One can start from French Lake, which is 24 miles east of the McAlpine Lake Portage. The course may include visits to Cirrus and Beaverhouse Lakes. A favoured route meriting further description follows.

ROUTE 4A

Jean Lake, from the northern entrance, east and then south, leads past campsites on opposite points to a rocky ledge at the bottom of the lake.

3 MILES. A new route leaves the southwest corner by a creek to Ceph Lake and down a stream to a large bay of Burntside Lake. Birchbark scrolls were found in a cave near here. A porcupine denned in another cave.

1½ MILES. *Rouge Lake* widens from a narrow channel to a small lake where Jean Creek leaves its waters. A small campsite by a rock ledge overlooks the waterfall. Fuel wood is at a premium here and the folding saw comes in handy. Black-winged dragonflies and bald eagles provide contrast in size; the same ratio exists between the size of the prey.

115 YARDS. Portage around the rapids to a marshy landing.

¼ MILE. Paddle through the white water lilies to a rocky falls about two feet high.

4 YARDS. Liftover.

1¼ MILES. Down the grassy creek, lift over a beaver dam and through a gap in another beaver dam.

75 YARDS. Portage on left side.

Jean Creek should not be difficult to travel during years when the water is fairly high but in dry season it might require more portaging. Two 220-yard portages can be used.

3¼ MILES. Jean Creek empties into a reedy bay and the route connects with the Dawson Trail at the head of Maligne River. From here to French Lake campsite is a 33-mile paddle with only two portages to cross.

CANOE ROUTE NO. 5: AGNES LAKE LOOP

AREA: Basswood Lake to Kawnipi Lake
TIME: 2 days, one way
DISTANCE: 24 miles of paddling; 2 miles of portages

This is also an easy route for beginners.

This could well be called the Boy Scout Trail. During the summer months, you will meet many a group of these enthusiastic paddlers. The route provides a pleasant side trip or the means of dividing the Hunter's Island trip into a series of shorter trips.

462 YARDS. *Bayley Bay* on the north shore of Basswood Lake has a fine sand beach near the ranger's cabin. Sand also has been packed on the good trail which leads past an excellent campsite and over a few slopes to a sandy landing.

1¼ MILES. *Burke Lake* offers a choice of two routes north. The *northwest* arm leads to a creek with two portages into North Bay from which two routes again can be taken northward—one through West, Shade, Noon, Summer and Silence Lakes to Agnes Lake, the other to the Kahshahpiwi Chain. The main route to Agnes, up the *northeast* arm of Burke Lake, leads to a good campsite.

30 YARDS. This short portage is on the north side of a creek flowing into Burke Lake.

2¼ MILES. *Sunday Lake*, and choice of two good campsites for a day of rest.

1,710 YARDS. The portage begins in a little bay on the east side of Sunday Lake. The path is very rocky and uneven and muddy in several places. Four canoe rests are passed before the rocky landing is reached. Fireplaces indicate this has been used as a camp-grounds. The map says this portage is 880 yards but we favour our pacing.

⅛ MILE. In and out is all the canoeing necessary in *Meadows Lake*.

770 YARDS. This portage seems shorter than would appear from the map as it is mainly downhill over a rough rocky path from and to good landings.

15 MILES. *Agnes Lake*, one of the most interesting waterways in Quetico Park, deserves detailed description.

1 MILE. *Louisa Lake* empties over the 30-foot drop of Louisa Falls into Agnes Lake on the east shore. Halfway up the falls is a basin in the rock, deep as a bath tub, a novel place for a refreshing dip on a hot day. There is a campsite here and another a short distance up.

1 MILE FURTHER. The greatest depth of water known in the Quetico, 285 feet, was measured here.

1 MILE ON. At the tip of this island is a faint pictograph of a canoe with two occupants.

1 MILE. *The Narrows*, where granitic ridges tower to shade the paddler. Lichens and mosses, orange, green, grey and black, cover the precipitous cliffs. Impressive, even awe-inspiring when storm clouds box the channel, this split in the volcanic mass will be remembered.

2 MILES. There is a campsite on a narrow point.

2½ MILES. Another campsite is seen on the west shore by the Portage to Silence Lake. North by a few canoe lengths the primitive painters must have passed, the evidence being two snowshoe hares in faded red and close by the most unusual aboriginal art in the Park—four white deer pecked into the rock surface.

1½ MILES N.E. Near the north end of an island is a good-sized campsite.

½ MILE N. Indian paintings are set low on the face of a cliff at the southeast end of an island whose length runs back northwest.

1 MILE. There is a campsite on the east side of the big island.

1¼ MILES. Another campsite is found on a small island opposite to the entrance to the East Channel route. Here wind,

NORTH A FEW CANOE LENGTHS THE PRIMITIVE PAINTERS MUST HAVE PASSED

time or some other factor will determine your choice of one of the three routes to Kawnipi Lake.

ROUTE 5(A): EAST CHANNEL ROUTE

Paddle northeast into a long narrow bay. A good campsite is on the north shore just west of the north arm of the bay. Near the entrance to the southerly arm you must follow is an old Indian grave. Once the box was on posts but it has now collapsed.

440 YARDS. Portage over glacial boulders and mud.

1¼ MILES. *Bird Lake* has a campsite on an island, not shown on the map. The portage from the lake begins at a beaver dam—rough, muddy at the start and ending at a rocky shallow landing below the rapids.

1¼ MILES. *Anubis Lake*: one wonders how the name of the dog-faced god of Egypt was given to a Canadian lake. There are walleyes here.

198 YARDS. Rocks and a shoal make the landing for the portage

poor but, spurred on by the mosquitoes, the fair trail is soon crossed.

1/16 MILE. A small pond is quickly crossed.

110 YARDS. A downhill portage. You are now 65 feet below the surface of Agnes Lake. A sign aids in finding this portage when you are coming from Kawnipi Lake.

1¾ MILES. *McVicar Bay* runs north to the island campsites on Kawnipi.

ROUTE 5(B): WEST CHANNEL ROUTE

1¾ MILES. Head north, keeping to the left of the big island.

154 YARDS. Portage into Agnes River.

1½ MILES. *Agnes River* narrows to a rapids.

175 YARDS. Portage on the right.

390 YARDS. Another new portage on the right.

300 YARDS. Portage on the left.

40 YARDS. A short portage into Murdoch Lake.

2 MILES. Murdoch Lake offers more opportunities to fishermen. A short portage around a rapids may be necessary.

1¼ MILES. A long bay is traversed to the Kawnipi route.

ROUTE 5(C): KEEWATIN LAKE ROUTE

Head north as in 5(B) but instead of entering the bay leading to the West Channel, paddle northwest to a bay at the most northerly end of Agnes Lake.

396 YARDS. Portage.

½ MILE. Cross a small unnamed lake.

462 YARDS. Portage.

1¼ MILES. *Keel Lake.* The Williams Lake route from Kahshahpiwi enters this lake by a stream on the western shore. Halfway up the west shore are pictographs, including three thunderbirds. This lake is now called Keewatin Lake.

462 YARDS. A clear but somewhat rocky portage follows the unnavigable water course.

2 MILES. Island campsite southwest of Rosie Island.

CANOE ROUTE NO. 6: THE KAHSHAHPIWI CHAIN

TIME: 2 days, one way

DISTANCE: 22 miles of paddling; 4,462 yards of portages

Some previous experience on canoe trips is recommended.

This is a favourite route of many canoeists. Waterways fan out in all directions from the lakes along the great geological fault which runs approximately north-northeast for eighteen miles.

The starting point chosen, and there are many choices as the map will show, is North Bay on Basswood Lake.

½ MILE. Follow the stream from the northeast corner of North Bay. There is a 50-yard portage along the stream.

½ MILE. Go east along the north shore of this unnamed lake.

66 YARDS. A short portage.

½ MILE. *West Lake* is long and very narrow. Head for the north.

50 YARDS. Another short portage.

¼ MILE. This unnamed lake is what most travellers would call a pond.

¼ MILE. Follow the stream and hope the beaver have not dammed it.

22 YARDS. There is a short portage, practically a liftover.

½ MILE. *Shade Lake* looks big after the lakes just crossed. The landing to look for is almost straight north from where you enter the lake.

440 YARDS. Portage to an unnamed lake.

¼ MILE. Maybe less; hardly time to get the bottom of the canoe wet.

704 YARDS. Over the hill and faraway, said someone of this portage.

½ MILE. *Grey Lake* offers a campsite.

528 YARDS. This portage will increase your appetite. Actually the trail is good.

1 MILE. Head for the northeast end of *Yum Yum Lake*, especially in wet years. The 1,210-yard portage from the northerly bay at the other end of the lake can be very mucky before the hill to Kahshahpiwi is reached.

110 YARDS. This portage from Yum Yum is good.

½ MILE. There is a good campsite on this unnamed lake.

150 YARDS. Portage from a little bay over a rise to a landing by the stream.

1¼ MILES. *McNiece Lake* is traversed to the westerly end.

900 YARDS. This is a new portage, high and dry, and it passes by one of the largest black ash in the northern woods. A man cannot encircle this ash with his arms.

4 MILES. Kahshahpiwi Lake has several campsites and offers excellent angling opportunities. At the north end of the lake is a stream which leads to the next lake.

½ MILE. The course is north across this unnamed lake.

150 YARDS. A downhill portage to Keefer Lake.

3 MILES. *Keefer Lake* has a good campsite. The east bay at the upper end of the lake is almost blocked by an island and the landing is north of this.

418 YARDS. Portage by the unnavigable stream.

3 MILES. *Sark Lake* expands westward and numerous islands and points tempt fishermen to stop a while. The course is up a long narrow channel.

462 YARDS. Portage by a rapids.

3 MILES. *Cairn Lake* is a long and narrow lake.

110 YARDS. Portage by a rapids.

½ MILE. Down the narrow stream.

220 YARDS. Portage round a rapids.

132 YARDS. Another rapids and another portage.

1¾ MILES. A long narrow channel, regarded as a bay of Kawnipi Lake, leads to an island campsite where this route joins the Back Trail route.

Few of the portages on this route are marked but they are easily found. Here are healing solitudes, fresh air, restful nights, and an opportunity to relax, all waiting to be enjoyed.

CANOE ROUTE NO. 7: THE MAN CHAIN

TIME: 2 days one way
DISTANCE: 21¼ miles of paddling; 1,903 yards of portages

Another easy route for beginners.

Practically paralleling the border route from Carp to Saganaga Lake, the Man Chain offers a visit to less frequented waters. We start from a position two miles north of the portage around Silver Falls where there is a campsite on a long peninsula jutting into Saganagons Lake.

½ MILE. Go southerly on the west side of the peninsula, crossing to the far shore.

¼ MILE. The shallow creek to Slate Lake is barred by fallen trees so head for the little bay just north.

56 YARDS. Easily seen, this portage goes up a slight grade to a rocky ledge.

¾ MILE. *Slate Lake* is crossed to a stream in the south bay.

½ MILE. Follow the river channel up through white and yellow water lilies.

1 MILE. Cross *Fran Lake* with its surprising echoes to the southwest end and go up the stream to a rapids.

308 YARDS. The portage starts at a stony landing in mucky water, goes up a steep grade and then finally 30 yards down a slope to a fine rocky landing.

¼ MILE. Cross the pond to the west end.

124 YARDS. An uphill portage by the creek flowing out of Bell Lake has fair rock landings on both ends. One could camp at the upper end.

1¾ MILES. *Bell Lake*, long and narrow, has very abrupt cliffs on the north side. This lake is like an oven on a hot day.

88 YARDS. This portage, over the hill and down again, is muddy

THIS LAKE IS LIKE AN OVEN ON A HOT DAY

60

at both ends and seems forty yards longer than the map indicates.

½ MILE. *Bit Lake* is left at a southeast bay.

22 YARDS. Portage straight uphill to a fair landing.

½ MILE. Unnamed lake of very dirty water, possibly the result of a broken beaver dam.

132 YARDS. The portage starts up a precipitous slope, then is boggy where poles have been laid to improve conditions. The landing is at a rock ledge into clear, deep water.

1¼ MILES. *Other Man Lake* is crystal clear and said to contain lake trout. About a quarter-mile from the west end are three campsites, one high on a hill having a crane fireplace, tables and a path to a dock.

150 YARDS. The portage is fairly level.

5 MILES. *This Man Lake*, long and narrow, has two good campsites, one on an island 3 miles down the lake. The slate roofing and asbestos sides of a mining company storehouse at the southwest end of the lake can be seen for 2 miles, an unpleasant sight in the otherwise unspoiled surroundings.

200 YARDS. The portage goes up a slight rise and then down a steep slope. Near the foot of the hill, a trail leads to an old cabin and a spring. The water flows out of an old iron pipe—beautiful, clear, cold water, the finest drink on a hot day.

½ MILE. *No Man Lake* is soon crossed.

½ MILE. A sandy-bottomed stream is easily followed, dodging low windfalls on the way.

2¾ MILES. *That Man Lake* shows evidence of mining activities formerly carried on in this section of the Park. A mile along the north shore are several buildings erected by a mining company seeking iron ore. A campsite is on an island just to the east. Maps of a few decades ago show that this lake was called Sarpedon, after the Lycian prince and son of Zeus who was killed by Patroclus in the Trojan war. Certainly this lake has had strange names.

748 YARDS. Portage downhill, parallel to the creek, to a low and muddy landing.

¼ MILE. *Sheridan Lake* is the place to try your lake trout lures.

76 YARDS. Portage from the rocky landing in the southeast bay down the hill to an excellent campsite on Carp Lake. The stream gurgles merrily close by and red-backed voles nest on the hillside. Another fine campsite is on the island opposite the end of the portage.

A short trip from here to Emerald Lake and back is worth taking. Head east along the north shore of Carp Lake for about two miles and into a narrow bay. The portage is about 400 yards long and the lake is regarded as a jewel by both anglers and lovers of the wilderness. An excellent campsite is on the south shore.

4 MILES. Carp Lake to Carp Portage on the Grand Portage Route.

CANOE ROUTE NO. 8: HUNTER'S ISLAND ROUTE

TIME: three weeks to a month

DISTANCE: 128 miles around Hunter's Island; total distance 185 miles

Actually surrounded by water, this vast island in the Quetico can be circumnavigated by following the Dawson Trail to Lac La Croix, the Grand Portage Route back to Saganaga Lake, and the Back Trail Route to Sturgeon Lake. When back at French Lake you will have many thrilling memories of the historic gateways to the West.

CANOE ROUTE NO. 9: KAMINISTIQUIA ROUTE

AREA: Thunder Bay to Baril Portage

TIME: 1 to 3 weeks

DISTANCE: 100 miles by water; 8½ miles by land

For experienced canoemen interested in travelling a historic route. Definitely not a pleasure cruise. Power dams have greatly altered conditions both above and below their sites.

Daniel Greysolon, Sieur Dulhut, built a fort in 1679 on the Mission, one of the three mouths of the Kaministiquia River. *Coureurs de bois* allied with him likely paddled upstream to use the river route that became the first gateway to the Canadian West. Jacques de Noyon travelled its waters to Rainy Lake in 1688. Later the fort was abandoned but in 1717 Zacharie Robutel, Sieur de la Noüe, re-established the post which was maintained until the closing days of New France. Only the burned timbers remained in 1767.

Roderic McKenzie "re-discovered" the route in 1798 and when the North West Company decided to move from Grand Portage, they built on the north bank of the Kaministiquia opposite an Indian village about a mile upstream. Bruyere is believed to have surveyed and laid out the post in 1802 and the move was completed at the cost of £10,000. On July 31, 1807, it was named Fort William to honour William McGillivray, then one of the outstanding partners of the North West Company. The XY Company had erected buildings near the "New Fort," but in 1804 the two firms amalgamated.

This ended the conflict among the Canadian traders and resulted in greater profits for the partners. Wages for first-year clerks were reduced from £100 to £60 a year and liquor sales to Indians fell from 19,400 to 13,500 gallons in one year. Goods at Fort William were sold at advances of 45 to 130 per cent over Montreal prices and at higher advances further west. In 1805, furs sent from the North West included 51,033 muskrat, 40,440 marten, 4,011 fine marten, 2,132 common otter, 4,328 mink, 2,268 fisher and 77,500 beaver skins.

The old Grand Portage Route attracted free traders and in 1806, Dominic Rousseau of Montreal entered into a partnership with a Mr. Delorme, whom he despatched from Montreal with two canoes to trade in the west. Alexander McKay, a "Nor'Wester," followed Delorme over Grand Portage and felled trees across the portages and narrow creeks that had to be crossed. Delorme left his trade goods in the forest and went to the "New Fort" where McGillivray ignored his appeals. The adventure had to be abandoned. Rousseau sued but finally settled out of court for the price of the goods at Montreal.

Methods similar to this and the influence the firm had in the courts of Lower Canada discouraged independent traders.

Ross Cox wrote, in 1817, "The buildings at Fort William consist of a large house, in which the dining-hall is situated, and in which the gentleman in charge resides; the council-house; a range of snug buildings for the accommodation of the people from the interior; a large counting-house; the doctor's residence; extensive stores for the merchandise and furs; a forge; various work-shops, with apartments for the mechanics, a number of whom are always stationed here. There is also a prison for refractory voyageurs. The whole is surrounded by wooden fortifications, flanked by bastions, and is sufficiently strong to withstand any attack from natives. Outside the fort is a shipyard, in which the Company's vessels on the lake are built and repaired. . . . The dining-hall is a noble apartment, and sufficiently capacious to entertain two hundred. A finely executed bust of the late Simon M'Tavish is placed in it, with portraits of various proprietors. . . . At the upper end of the hall, there is a very large map of the Indian country, drawn

A FINELY EXECUTED BUST OF THE LATE SIMON MCTAVISH

with great accuracy by Mr. David Thompson, astronomer to the Company, and comprising all their trading-posts, from Hudson's Bay to the Pacific Ocean, and from Lake Superior to Athabasca and Great Slave Lake."

New conflicts were brewing. The Earl of Selkirk gained control of the Hudson's Bay Company and started a settlement in the Red River valley to provide homes for Scottish crofters who had lost their lands. The North West Company now fought their rivals with organized vandalism. Crops were trampled, barns burnt, and shots fired from the bushes.

Matters came to a head in 1816. Colin Robertson hired *voyageurs* in Montreal and, using what the North West Company regarded as their own highway, took trade goods up the Kaministiquia and west to Athabasca; this was the first time Hudson's Bay Company goods had not come through Hudson Bay. Violence erupted. Cuthbert Grant led a group of half-breeds against the settlers, and in the massacre of Seven Oaks on June 19th, Governor Semple and twenty-one others were killed. This slaughter took place near Main Street of the Winnipeg of today. Meanwhile Selkirk was moving up the lakes with a party of a hundred settlers recruited from the disbanded ranks of the Regiment de Meuron. Hearing of the massacre, he set out for Fort William. Arranging his men and artillery to command the approaches to the fort, he soon took possession of the place. McGillivray and other Nor'Westers were arrested and sent east for trial on charges of "High Treason, Conspiracy and Murder." Soon they were free on bail and swearing out warrants for Selkirk's arrest. Selkirk established a camp at Point de Meuron, nine miles up the broad river. In the spring, he went west to reorganize his colony. Both Selkirk and the North West Company suffered financially as a result of the discord. The aggressive competition ended with the union of the two firms in 1821.

Following this event, York boats brought the trade goods from Hudson Bay to Fort Garry and in 1836 Washington Irving wrote, "The feudal state of Fort William is at an end; its council chamber is silent and deserted; its banquet hall no longer echoes to the burst of loyalty, or the 'auld world' ditty;

the lords of the lakes and forests have passed away." Today, the old fort has disappeared but the streets of the progressive city of Thunder Bay bear the names of many of the famous fur-traders who dined in the great banquet hall.

A letter from Catherine Moodie Vickers to her mother, the authoress Susanna Moodie, described a trip made on August 21, 1873. "Three miles above Point de Meuron at the entrance to Slate River, where John has a large amount of land, the scenery is beautiful beyond description; on our left, Slate River dashing down through mountains of slate among the beautiful little islands of the Kaministiquia, McKay's mountain behind us, the roaring rapids in front of us, and a beautiful natural meadow on our right with tall elm trees like a plantation, the dense forest rising behind. The greenness of this part of the country is something wonderful. . . . After passing these islands the business of poling the canoe began."

The demi-portage, 924 feet long, is Paresseux or Lazy portage. Nine miles upstream Mountain Portage led around the 119.5 foot barrier of Kakabeka Falls. Harmon recorded in his journal, July 15, 1805: "The North West Company have here a storehouse, to which they send provisions &c., from the New Fort, . . . the river from this to that place is generally shallow, and is full of rapids. Those, therefore, who are going into the interior, cannot take a full load, until they arrive at this place; and here they usually take their supply of provisions."

Paul Kane, who sketched Kakabeka Falls, May 25, 1846, expressed his opinion that the "falls surpass even those of Niagara in picturesque beauty," and Mrs. Vickers wrote: "Gilded and burnished by the morning sun the great current of water came rushing down nearly two hundred feet, the whole breadth of the river, no island or stone to break the outline— one pure torrent of snow-white foam, not clear or crystalline, but like a continuous mass of cream. As it reaches the rapids below it breaks over the rocks, which, from the quantity of iron in the neighbourhood, are bright red. . . . There is a little island . . . and here we landed . . . we were in the loveliest rainbow—the stones, the trees, everything gloriously colored with it."

Mountain Portage now passes through the Kakabeka Provincial Park. Hard-packed by the moccasined feet of the
voyageurs, the lower end of the trail can still be traced, but
above it is hidden by gravel and highway and a power dam.
Kane listed the portages around the many rapids above Kakabeka: Lost Men's Portage, Pin (Knifestone) Portage, Ecarte
Portage, Rose Décharge, De l'Isle Portage, Recousi and Couteau
portages, Belanger, Mauvais, Tremble and Penet Décharge,
Maitre, Little Dog, Dog, and Big Dog portages. Today, a hydro-
electric power plant at Silver Falls has greatly altered conditions along the river.

Dog Lake Portage, 3,181 yards long, was a stiff climb from
either direction. There is a legend that the Sioux dug clay from
a high point on the hill and the shape of a dog was evident
when they filled the hollows with sand. This was said to have
been done to taunt the Ojibwa whom they had defeated.

Dog Lake, twelve miles long, was welcomed by west-bound
voyageurs who threw away the poles used in ascending the
Kaministiquia River before they crossed the last portage. It
was on lakes like this that observant travellers noted that the
North canoemen made sixty strokes a minute with great regu-
larity. Very small paddles with the blades painted red were
used. The Indian, more concerned with his immediate surroundings, paddled slowly and used very wide-bladed paddles.

The *voyageurs*, picked for their ability and health, paddled
and portaged from fifteen to eighteen hours a day, and, with
lungs as untiring as their arms, sang "La belle rose blanche"

THE NORTH CANOEMEN MADE SIXTY STROKES A MINUTE

and other songs as they sped across the waters. The prevalent costume was a red woollen cap, a short shirt, a breech cloth, long leggings of tanned deerhide and moccasins. A long, gay sash (*ceinture flèche*) was tied around the waist with the fringed ends dangling near the knees.

Dog River, winding among banks of sand, enters at the northwest corner of the lake. L'Abbé Belcourt remarked in 1831, "The Rivière des Chiens is very torturous and its waters very dirty. We made in one part nearly half a league to repass ten feet from where we had passed before." A dam at the foot of Dog Lake has raised the water level and created floating islands of vegetation during high-water periods.

Little Rapids, a demi-portage; the 66-yard Barrier Portage; and the 154-yard carry around Portage du Jordain lie upstream. R. Ballantyne mentioned spruce grouse caught here with a running noose on a branch. Dog River is left and Prairie Creek, narrow and winding, is followed to Muddy or Viscous Lake. Today, a private road which leaves Highway 17 just west of Linko crosses Prairie Creek.

A portage of two canoe lengths leads into Cold Water Lake. This clear, shallow pool, long called L'Eau Froide, is fed by a copious spring whose waters are reputed too cold to drink.

Prairie Portage, a two and a quarter mile carry, crosses the height of land into Rupert's Land. David Thompson recorded the distance as 4,566 yards and called it Meadow Portage. Here Hugh Faries, on July 7, 1804, "met Mr. Roderick Mckenzie & 2 other Gentlemen of the same Name. They had tea with us and departed."

When a *voyageur* reached the end of this portage he would be glad to remove the tump line from his forehead. Placing the 180-pound load of two pieces in the canoe he would straighten his back, brush the flies from his long hair, and dog trot back to pick up his next load. The carry completed, he would likely smoke his clay pipe for ten minutes and then pipe, flint and steel would join the tobacco in his beaded pouch; refreshed, he would take his position in the canoe.

Lac La Prairie is only a quarter-mile hike. Milieu Portage, a level half-mile through a swamp where pitcher plant and

Labrador tea are common, leads to Lac du Milieu, formerly Lac du Savanne. A mile to the southwest, the canoes had to be unloaded again. Great Savanne Portage, 2,662 yards long, "consists of a wet tamarack swamp, in which moss grows everywhere to the depth of one foot or eighteen inches, the moss is supported by a retentive buff clay." In the days of the North West Company, a causeway of hewn logs, three abreast, provided good footing, but in 1830 Frances Simpson referred to it as "formed of a bridge of Logs in a very crazy, & decayed state, so slippery, unsteady & uneven, as to occasion the greatest difficulty in crossing it."

The Savanne River, entered just below a rapid, is followed for eighteen miles through low, marshy banks. Frances Simpson's canoe journal reads: "Descended the river Embarras . . . which takes its name from the frequent obstructions of wind fallen timber, which is carried down by the Spring floods; requiring the constant use of the axe to cut a passage through it." Highway 17 now crosses the winding Savanne River which flows into Lac des Mille Lacs.

Twenty-two miles across island-studded Lac des Mille Lacs is Baril Portage, where the Kaministiquia and Dawson Routes become one, following the same trail through Quetico Park.

CANOE ROUTE NO. 10: THE OLIFAUNT LOOP

A combination of the Bisk-Beg-Bud chain to Olifaunt Lake, over the portage to Sturgeon Lake and back by the Deux Rivières and Pine portages to French Lake. The whole route has been described in the Dawson Trail and Back Trail logs. The route is an easy one for beginners. This trip has been made in three days but for real enjoyment spend a week on the way. By water: 41 miles; by land: 3,264 yards.

CANOE ROUTE NO. 11: WESTERN BORDER ROUTE

This trip, for the experienced canoeist, moves along the less frequented western border of Quetico Park, and passes over an area once logged by the Shevlin-Clarke Lumber Co. Ltd.

Cirrus Lake can be reached by a 924-yard portage from Kasakokwog Lake or by a new 100-yard portage in the bay east of the dam north of Eden Isle in Quetico Lake. Two portages, 198 yards and 880 yards are on the way to Beaverhouse Lake. Down the Quetico River are seven portages of 200 yards or less, while up the Namakan River are three portages of 150, 200 and 265 yards. The last is opposite the Indian village site. You can choose your course back to your embarkation point. Time: 1 week, one way. By water: 50 miles; by land 5,231 yards.

CANOE ROUTE NO. 12: HERON BAY—CAMEL LAKE—KEATS LAKE CUT-OFF

This provides a connection between the Dawson and Back Trail routes for those who have not time to follow either route all the way. Just below Sturgeon Narrows, head southerly into Heron Bay and on into Fred Lake. Portage 484 yards into Cutty Creek; portage 44 yards to Nan Lake and follow the creek into Camel Lake. Portage 154 yards along the creek out of Camel Lake; and 66 yards from the creek into Eag Lake. There is a 44-yard portage along the creek from Eag to Cub Lake and a 66-yard hike along the creek between Cub and Baird lakes. A 902-yard portage leads from Baird to Keats Lake. This route was cleared out by a portage crew during the summer of 1957. Time: 1 day or less, one way. By water: 12 miles; by land: 1,826.

CANOE ROUTE NO. 13: DARKY TO JOYCE LAKE TRIP

Beaver are blamed for mucky conditions on this route from the Dawson Trail to Minn Lake. The map shows optional trails from Tanner Lake, Rebecca Falls, and Crooked Lake. Follow Darky River to Darky Lake to see the finest of the Painted Rocks in the Park—along the east shore at the southern end of the lake. Then cross to Brent, Suzanette and Burt lakes. When entering the latter, look for the Painted Hands on the east shore cliffs. On to Marj and Joyce (what walleyes haunt these waters!) to the Kahshahpiwi Chain and back to French Lake—an unforgettable trip of great variety. Time: 3 days, one way. By water: 31 miles; by land: 4,338 yards.

CANOE ROUTE NO. 14: McKENZIE LAKE LOOP

Leave the Back Trail at McKenzie Bay and portage into the lake. About the centre of the north shore is a 100-yard trail to a small nameless lake; cross this to another 100-yard portage into Lindsay Lake. Look at your map and see what lies ahead —two portages each over 1½ miles long: rugged and recommended only for those in good condition. This trip should be made when water levels are high as travel in Baptism Creek can be difficult in dry years. Time: 2 to 3 days, one way. By water: 26 miles; by land: 6,292 yards.

CANOE ROUTE NO. 15: THE POACHER'S ROUTE

This is seldom travelled, and is for experienced adventurers. It is an old Indian trail between the now abandoned Ojibwa encampment on Kawa Bay and the conjuring grounds reported at Shebandowan Lake. During the years beaver trapping was closed this route was used by fur poachers seeking an illicit fortune in pelts. Time: 3 days, one way. By water: 66 miles; by land: 8 portages.

Embarking where the Kashabowie River leaves Lake Shebandowan, one should paddle southwest to the lower end of Upper Shebandowan Lake and follow the unnamed stream to a lake that looks like an inverted V on the map. A long portage into Skimpole Lake and another 800 yards long brings one to Burchell, formerly Round Lake. An excellent motor road connects this lake with the highway between Port Arthur and Atikokan. The road skirts the Coldstream Copper Mine property. Long known as the Tip Top mine, during World War I it produced rich ore which was hauled over a narrow gauge railroad to a Canadian National Railways spur. Burchell's sandy beaches attract hundreds of campers to the undeveloped provincial park campsite along its northern shore. The majority of canoeists will likely prefer to start this trip from here.

Four miles across Burchell Lake (where big lake trout lurk) is a 732-yard portage over a steep hill into Hermia Lake. Four miles down a winding creek is Snodgrass Lake. A truck road from Burchell Lake crosses the old portage to Moss Lake on its way to Moss, now Ardeen Gold Mine. Originally the Jack Fish Lake Mine, this was the first gold mine in northwestern Ontario. Walpole Roland wrote: "The Indians, . . . Jean Baptiste and Michel Pouchette, who were in the employ of Mr. Neil Whyte, of the Hudson Bay Company's post at Beau-Blanc, found this vein on a return trip from Fort William in the winter of 1870–71. Mr. Whyte forwarded specimens from this vein to Mr. P. McKellar." Peter McKellar, later founder and benefactor of the Thunder Bay Historical Society, followed the route just described in 1871 and mining operations began in January, 1872. The ore contained copper and iron pyrites, galena, zinc blende, gold, sylvanite and tellurium. "A road was grubbed out between Lake Shebandowan and the mine. . . . However, the Indians had not at their period relinquished their claim to this section of country, and it is recorded that the notorious Indian chief, Blackstone, with his warriors, arrived at the mine towards the end of March, and requested the entire party to leave until satisfactory arrangements had been made between his band and the government."

The Poacher's Route leaves Snodgrass Lake at the southwest arm by a portage around a falls. Below the gorge the winding Wawaig River leads past tamarack swamps and jackpine ridges to Kawa Bay. Two portages on the right bank by-pass falls and a long portage on the left leads by a rapids. The slow moving waters of the lower Wawaig River channel flow through a favourite forage ground for moose. Today towering birch and poplar rise from within the remains of the cabin walls of the

A FAVOURITE FORAGE GROUND FOR MOOSE

ancient Indian village. Here the Kakawiagamak Indian Reserve, 24C, had been established by the North West Angle Treaty of 1873. Both Ontario and Manitoba claimed the lands around the Reserve; in fact, Manitoba claimed their provincial boundary should be just east of the new City of Thunder Bay! Finally the Privy Council established the present provincial boundaries in 1884. Soon after this an outbreak of smallpox caused most of the survivors to flee westward. Bob Readman, the first warden of the Quetico Forest Reserve, recalls seeing remnants of an old trading post and a flagpole on the north bank of the Waweig River in 1906. The reservation was almost abandoned at that time. Three or four families, living in birch-bark teepees, were smoking moose meat.

The 5948-acre Reserve was abolished by a provincial Act in 1915. Evidently a few Ojibwa continued to live there at times for there is a report that the influenza epidemic of 1918–19 hit hard at Kawa Bay. A grave on Agnes Lake, with a roof-like low structure over it, is said to be that of a Chief Blackstone who died while trying to obtain help for his band.

Back to the map – you can see countless variations of the trips described. During the past ten years Park portage crews have cut a multitude of new portages into numerous small lakes, especially in the northwest portion of the Park. Some old portages have been improved. You can choose your own vagabond trail. The Park Superintendent, Ministry of Natural Resources, Atikokan, Ontario, P0T 1C0, will be glad to answer any inquiry concerning routes not described as well as answer other questions that may arise. The map is your passport to the finest vacation land in North America – Quetico Provincial Park.

The Quetico Park Visitor Distribution Programme necessitates reservations be made by anyone planning on camping in the interior of the Park. Write early for advance reservations to:

> Reservations
> Quetico Provincial Park
> Atikokan, Ontario
> P0T 1C0

Before the White Man Came

THE sharp-eyed canoeman, as he paddles beneath the overhanging cliffs which mark the shorelines of Darky, Agnes and other lakes, will feel the thrill of discovery when he first becomes aware of man-made pictures on the rocks. There are a good many of these in Quetico and they seem to represent a variety of objects, including men, the sun, the moon, canoes and different types of birds and animals. Most have been painted on the rock surfaces with a mixture of hematite and fish oil; a few have been chipped or crudely engraved on the rocks. Archaeologists call the former pictographs and the latter petroglyphs.

Who drew these unusual pictures? When were they painted or carved? What do they mean? These questions have not yet been answered with certainty, though many conjectures have been made. The pictures are not recent and no Indian now living can explain them satisfactorily. Some, which include representations of firearms, must have been executed within the past three hundred years. It is assumed that many of the others must be centuries older. Experts are now attempting to shed light on these mysteries and they may possibly conclude that some of the symbols have religious associations and that others are simply messages or records of events which were of special importance to the artists.

The rock paintings are especially fascinating, but they are not the only clues the camper may come across of Quetico's ancient inhabitants. There are the records of the campsites, the tell-tale chips of flint, the bits of crude pottery, the pieces of slate and occasionally copper which, when analysed by archaeologists, give us a clearer picture of human life in the region during centuries long passed. We know, for instance, that people were wandering through Quetico five thousand years ago. They were nomads who travelled in small groups, living off the land as best they could, collecting the wild fruits of the forest, and fishing and hunting with simple tools and weapons.

Coming closer to the present day in time, we also know, through the work of archaeologists, that the Cree Indians, who now live in the woodlands to the north, and the Dakota-Sioux and Assiniboine, who today are Plains Indians, also roamed through the Quetico. However, by the time the first French explorers reached the region in the seventeenth century, the tribe we know as the Ojibwa or Chippewa was beginning to dominate the region. These early shiftings of tribal groups were gradual and were likely related to the quest for food. That they sometimes involved bloodshed is clear too from the records of the eighteenth-century travellers, who were themselves not immune from danger. La Vérendrye's son, Jean Baptiste, and Father Aulneau, the second missionary to pass through the Quetico, were killed along with nineteen *voyageurs* on Massacre Island in Lake of the Woods in June 1736, victims of the Dakota-Sioux. Even as late as 1857—just over a hundred years ago—George Gladman could report that the Ojibwa of Lac La Pluie were on the warpath against their traditional enemies, the Dakota-Sioux.

What sort of people were these early Indians, the Ojibwa, whom the first French travellers encountered? Their way of life differed radically from our own. They were not great in numbers, though they occupied a tremendous sweep of territory. They did not live in communities in our sense of the term. For the most of the year they lived in small family groups, geographically isolated one group from another except for a few weeks or a month or two in spring and early summer. In engaging in the struggle for existence, they were wonderfully adjusted to their environment. Indeed, they were an integral part of their environment and lived in a harmony—unknown to us—which blended together their own lives, the natural forces they could see and feel, and the supernatural world which, though invisible, they assumed to be near at hand.

The Ojibwa were campers *par excellence*—although they did not think of themselves in this way. They had several types of dwellings but all had a similar foundation framework of poles, driven into the ground and lashed with cross-pieces for support. Coverings consisted of woven rush mats or rolls of birchbark (banked in winter with poles, logs, earth and perhaps snow) to give the appearance of "teepees," wedge tents or dome-shaped dwellings.

Their tools and weapons were fashioned from materials close at hand. Wood, including bark and roots and rushes, provided bows and arrows, snares, twine, snowshoes, toboggans, food platters and storage containers (birchbark). Stone was equally useful: chert or flint was the source material for scrapers, knives, arrow and spear points; slate was chipped, ground and sometimes polished into axes and adzes. Awls and needles were fashioned from bone and some axes and adzes may have been pounded into shape from raw copper obtained from deposits such as those to be found on Isle Royale in Lake Superior.

A modern camper would find an Ojibwa canoe of great interest, for it was the prototype of many of the canoes which glide along our northern waters today. The Indian canoe-maker began by girdling one or more birch trees (depending on the girth of the trees and the amount of bark he needed) just above the roots and just below the lowest branches. He worked in the spring when the rising sap made the bark pliable and easy to peel off with wedges. Sheets of bark were stitched together and laid out on the ground, held in rough position by a supporting outer framework of stakes driven into the earth. An inner layer of cedar strips would be held in place by cedar boughs, fashioned into ribs and gunwales, all sewn carefully together with "wattap" (spruce roots). Waterproofing was done with hot spruce or balsam pitch. Cedar was also used for thwarts and paddles. The resulting canoe was light yet sturdy, responding easily to the paddler's thrust and twist yet capable of carrying astonishing loads. To an Ojibwa, the rivers and lakes were his highways and his canoe his means of transportation in all seasons except winter.

Clothing was usually made from the skins of the moose and the woodland caribou. The men wore breechcloths and long leggings while the women were clothed in dresses and shorter leggings. Both sexes wore moccasins. In winter, they wore coats woven from long strips of rabbit fur or robes consisting of five or six beaver skins sewn together with sinew, worn with the fur next to the body. Prime winter furs so worn for eighteen months later became known as "castor gras d'hiver" and were the most valuable to the hat-makers of Europe.

The Ojibwa were almost constantly on the move. It is recorded that some groups practised a limited agriculture but

ASTONISHING LOADS

most of them depended upon nature's harvests for their food. In winter, the family groups spread out over their hunting territories (and, after the arrival of white fur-traders, their trapping grounds) to snare rabbits and other small animals, to hunt the larger game animals with bow and arrow and to fish with spears through holes in the ice-covered lakes and rivers. In spring, the family groups would come together to collect and boil down the sap from the sugar maples into syrup and sugar. These provided a welcome touch of sweetness to the diet and the occasion marked the beginning of the brief communal social season. The summers were spent in fishing and gathering the wild berries as they ripened. Late summer saw the harvesting of wild rice, which, like maple syrup and fish, could be stored safely for use in winter. "Rock tripe"—a type of lichen—and the inner bark of certain trees also provided sustenance of a sort.

The Ojibwa were not a united people in our terms. The little bands or family groups were quite independent of one another politically, though they shared a common ancestry and had like traditions and language. There were also ties of blood, through their conventions of marriage, but the eternal search for food and the never-ending movement from region to region prevented the growth of large villages. Each group would have

77

its own leader, chosen by mutual consent for his abilities, and his term of office would last just as long as he continued to fulfil his functions satisfactorily.

Ojibwa children were allowed to play and were cherished and well loved by their parents. However, the harsh realities of northern woodland life dictated that the children begin preparing for adult life almost as soon as they could walk. Little girls began helping their mothers, learning by observation and practice the chores and skills of the wigwam household. Little boys followed their fathers into the bush, learning to stalk, to fish, to snare and to hunt. By the time a young couple married, probably in their late teens, they were trained to cope with the continuing problems of their unbending wilderness environment.

The Ojibwa could be described as a deeply religious people. The supernatural surrounded them on all sides in the form of "manitous," a word which has been translated—imperfectly—to mean both spirits and mysteries. These manitous lived in waterfalls and stones, in birds and animals and trees, in the sky—everywhere. There were evil ones and good ones, manitous to be placated, manitous to be thanked and manitous to be appealed to. Each youth had his own special manitou ("guardian angel") and all through his life he was deeply aware of the close and intense bond which linked him with the world of the manitous as well as with the rocks and waters, the birds and animals, which he could see around him. To help gain the intervention of good spirits and to ward off the evil intentions of bad spirits the Ojibwa had several types of medicine men. Some were conjurers, some were seers and prophets, others dealt only in herbal remedies. Some, who went through an elaborate apprenticeship to learn special rituals and herbal lore, were banded together into the Grand Medicine Society, or Midewiwin, a secret medicine society which had branches all through the northern woodland area.

Just over one hundred years ago, Professor Henry Youle Hind wrote (1857): "The great enemies to extended cultivation are the Lac La Pluie Indians. They are not only numerous but very independent and although diminishing in numbers, they frequently hold near Fort Frances their grand medicine ceremonies, at which 500 and 600 individuals sometimes assemble. The number of Indians visiting this fort, for purposes of trade, reaches 1500."

Simon J. Dawson, observing at this time also, said of these Indians, "The men are generally tall and well formed and some of the women remarkably comely." He mentioned the feast of the White Dog at the opening of navigation on the Rainy River.

Crooked Neck, a principal chief, opposed a treaty that was offered by the whites in 1870. Clad in breechcloth, his body painted yellow, he refused a proffered gift of a red shirt with the words, "Am I a pike to be caught with such bait as that? Shall I sell my land for a bit of red cloth? We will let the pale-faces pass through our country, but we will sell them none of our land, nor have any of them to live amongst us."

The tide of events was overwhelming, however, and on October 3, 1873, the North West Angle Treaty was signed. Under its terms, the Ojibwa gave up title to an area of 55,000 square miles, a region which included what we now know as Quetico Provincial Park.

Bibliography

THE list given below includes only a few of the books containing important references to the Quetico area. Material was obtained from other sources, including the *Canadian Historical Review*; the Wisconson Historical Collections; the *Jesuit Relations*; Geological Survey of Canada, *Reports of Progress*; Ontario Bureau of Mines, *Reports*; the Minnesota Historical Society; the Canadian Archives; the publications of the Thunder Bay Historical Society; and especially *The Beaver*, the quarterly publication of the Hudson's Bay Company, Winnipeg, Manitoba.

BELCOURT, Georges-Antoine. *Mon Itinéraire du lac des Deux-Montagnes à la Rivière Rouge.* Bulletin de la Société Historique de Saint-Boniface, vol. IV. Montréal 1913.

BIGSBY, John J. *The Shoe and Canoe; or, Pictures of Travel in the Canadas.* London, 1850.

BERTRAND, Joseph Placide. *Highway of Destiny.* New York: Vantage Press, 1959.

BURPEE, Lawrence J., editor. *Journals and Letters of Pierre Gaultier de Varennes de la Vérendrye and his Sons* (Publications of the Champlain Society, vol. XVI). Toronto, 1927.

CAMPBELL, Marjorie Wilkins. *The North West Company.* Toronto: Macmillan Company of Canada, Ltd., 1957.

COATSWORTH, Emerson S. *The Indians of Quetico.* Quetico Foundation Series, no. 1. Toronto: University of Toronto Press for the Foundation, 1957.

COUES, Elliott, editor. *New Light on the Early History of the Greater Northwest: The Manuscript Journals of Alexander Henry . . . and of David Thompson . . . 1799–1814.* Three vols. New York, 1897.

COX, Ross. *Adventures on the Columbia River, . . . Together with a Journey across the American Continent.* Two vols. London, 1831.

DAWSON, Simon J. In: Great Britain, Colonial Office, *Papers Relative to the Exploration of the Country between Lake Superior and the Red River Settlement.* London, 1859.

DELAFIELD, Major Joseph. *The Unfortified Boundary.* Edited by Robert McElroy and Thomas Riggs. New York, 1943.

FRANCHÈRE, Gabriel. *Narrative of a Voyage to the Northwest Coast of America in the Years 1811, 1812, 1813, and 1814.* Translated and edited by J. V. Huntington. New York, 1854.

GARRY, Nicholas. "Diary." In *Transactions of the Royal Society of Canada*, Second Series, vol. VII, Section II. Ottawa, 1900.

GATES, Charles M., editor. *Five Fur Traders of the Northwest: Being the Narrative of Peter Pond, and the Diaries of John Macdonell, Archibald N. McLeod, Hugh Faries, and Thomas Connor*. Minneapolis: University of Minnesota Press, 1933.

GRANT, George M. Ocean to Ocean. Toronto, 1873.

HARMON, Daniel W. *A Journal of Voyages and Travels in the Interior of North America*. Toronto, 1904.

HENRY, Alexander. *Travels and Adventures in Canada and the Indian Territories, between the Years 1760 and 1776*. Edited by James Bain. Toronto, 1901.

HIND, Henry Youle. *Narrative of the Canadian Red River Exploring Expedition of 1857 and of the Assiniboine and Saskatchewan Exploring Expedition of 1858*. Two vols. London, 1860.

HUYSHE, Captain G. L. *The Red River Expedition*. London, 1871.

INNIS, Harold A. *The Fur Trade in Canada: an Introduction to Canadian Economic History*. Revised ed. Toronto: University of Toronto Press, 1956.

JACQUES, Florence Page. *Canoe Country*. St. Paul: University of Minnesota Press, 1938. *Snowshoe Country*. St. Paul, 1944.

KANE, Paul. *Wanderings of an Artist among the Indians of North America*. London, 1859.

MACKENZIE, Alexander. *Voyages from Montreal through the Continent of North America to the Frozen and Pacific Oceans in 1789 and 1793, with an Account of the Rise and State of the Fur Trade*. New York, 1903.

MASSON, L.-R. *Les Bourgeois de la compaignie du Nord-Ouest*. Two vols. Québec, 1889–1890.

MEEN, V. B. *Quetico Geology*. Quetico Foundation Series, no. 2. Toronto; University of Toronto Press for the Foundation, 1959.

MORTON, Arthur S. *A History of the Canadian West to 1870–71*. Toronto, 1939.

NUTE, Grace Lee. *Caesars of the Wilderness*. New York, 1943. *Rainy River Country*. St. Paul, 1950. *The Voyageur*. St. Paul: Minnesota Historical Society, 1955. *The Voyageur's Highway*. St. Paul, 1941.

O'LEARY, Peter. *Travels and Experiences in Canada, the Red River territory, and the United States*. London, 1875.

STEVENS, James. *Paul Bunyan*. Garden City, N.Y., 1925.

TANNER, John. *A Narrative of the Captivity and Adventures of John Tanner*. Edited by Edwin James. New York, 1830.

TYRRELL, J. B., editor. *David Thompson's Narrative of His Explorations in Western America, 1784–1812*. Publications of the Champlain Society, vol. XII. Toronto: The Society, 1916.

WALLACE, W. Stewart, editor. *Documents Relating to the North West Company*. Publications of the Champlain Society, vol. XXII. Toronto: The Society, 1934.

——*The Pedlars of Quebec and Other Papers on the Nor'Westers*. . . . Toronto: Ryerson Press, 1954.

Remember!

BE CAREFUL WITH FIRE

Dr. A. P. Coleman of the Ontario Bureau of Mines wrote of a forest fire that swept from Atikokan to Lac des Milles Lac in August 1894: "So dense was the smoke that on even narrow lakes the canoe had to be steered by compass, unless one were content to coast slowly along the shore. On Baril Lake, August 29th, the air was so thick with smoke and falling ashes and cinders that it became dark at noon day, and we simply had to land and wait on the blackened, fire-ravaged shore till the worst of the gloom had been washed out of the air by a shower. The flare of blazing trees at night in the half choking atmosphere made one very careful to camp where the fire had already passed, leaving nothing more to burn. So furious was the conflagration that birds were killed in the air, and in the case of one small lake all the fish perished, and floated dead on the surface, when we passed a day or two later. Large trees are not burned completely by these fires, as a rule, but are generally killed, and in a very short time the blackened trunks are invaded by the larvae of *Monohammus confusor* or *M. Sentellatus*, which tunnel into the wood and destroy it. The ceaseless sound of their rasping horny jaws can be heard at times for a quarter of a mile away from these shadeless, funereal forests, and little heaps of sawdust soon accumulate at the foot of each tree."

BE CERTAIN YOUR FIRE IS OUT BEFORE YOU LEAVE THE CAMPSITE.

BE CAREFUL WITH INSECTS

Captain G. L. Huyshe, who served under Wolseley in 1870, wrote of the insects that occasionally can make life miserable if one is not prepared. "The black fly, however, bad as he is, is definitely preferable to the mosquito, for he is a gentleman and goes to bed at night, whereas the mosquito bullies the unhappy victim even more at night than in the daytime. . . . sandflies—their bite is as if you had been rubbed over with cayenne pepper; you feel a sudden burning, and have some difficulty in discovering the enemy, so diminutive is he. The French Canadians very aptly call them brûlot. The deer fly is a large mustard-coloured insect, three-quarters of an inch long, and furnished with nippers. He takes a piece of flesh right out when he bites."

BE CAREFUL—NOT CARELESS

"Safety First" is a good motto wherever you go.

Don't stand up in your canoe. Watch the weather. Take advantage of the portages. Use your axe sanely and correctly— the doctor is a long distance away.

EMERGENCY

A big smudge on the shore of a lake will attract the attention of Land and Forest patrol planes. Build a good fire, then heap on green boughs with the leaves on to make smoke. The letters S. O. S. can be made on a beach to confirm the emergency— they should be at least ten feet long. Other calls for help are given in a series of three: three lights, three whistles, etc. These should be answered by two signals of a similar nature.

Birds of Quetico

THE spice of life is found in the Quetico. Over two hundred species of birds have flown in the Park. Excellent birding awaits keen observers and those who know the songs of breeding birds. May is the exciting time though every season provides opportunities to enjoy this and other natural history hobbies. Quetico is a haven for Bald Eagles, Ospreys and Loons, birds typical of the wilderness.

The check list does not include unusual sight records: White Pelican, Swainson's Hawk, Peregrine Falcon, Caspian Tern, Red-headed Woodpecker and Yellow-headed Blackbird: or avifauna identified close to but not in the Park—Shoveler, White-winged Scoter, Common Scoter, Sharp-tailed Grouse, Sandhill Crane, Coot, Woodcock, Long-eared Owl, Black-billed Magpie, Varied Thrush, Bohemian Waxwing, Northern Shrike, Lark Bunting and Lark Sparrow.

SPRING AND FALL MIGRANTS

Horned Grebe
Whistling Swan
Canada Goose
Snow Goose
Pintail
Baldpate
Wood Duck
Greater Scaup
Rough-legged Hawk
Semipalmated Plover
Golden Plover
Black-bellied Plover
Greater Yellowlegs
Lesser Yellowlegs
Pectoral Sandpiper
White-rumped Sandpiper
Baird's Sandpiper

Least Sandpiper
Dunlin
Long-billed Dowitcher
Semipalmated Sandpiper
Sanderling
Northern Phalarope
Water Pipit
Orange-crowned Warbler
Blackpoll Warbler
Pine Grosbeak
Common Redpoll
Tree Sparrow
Harris Sparrow
White-crowned Sparrow
Fox Sparrow
Lapland Longspur
Snow Bunting

SUMMER VISITORS AND PERMANENT RESIDENTS

Common Loon
Red-necked Grebe
Pied-billed Grebe
Great Blue Heron
American Bittern
Mallard
Black Duck
Green-winged Teal
Blue-winged Teal
Lesser Scaup
Common Goldeneye
Hooded Merganser
Common Merganser
Red-breasted Merganser
Turkey Vulture
Goshawk
Sharp-shinned Hawk
Cooper's Hawk
Red-tailed Hawk
Bald Eagle
Broad-winged Hawk
Marsh Hawk
Osprey
Pigeon Hawk
Sparrow Hawk
Spruce Grouse
Ruffed Grouse
Sora
Killdeer
Common Snipe
Spotted Sandpiper
Solitary Sandpiper
Herring Gull
Ring-billed Gull
Belted Kingfisher
Yellow-shafted Flicker
Pileated Woodpecker
Yellow-bellied Sapsucker
Hairy Woodpecker
Downy Woodpecker
Black-backed 3-toed Woodpecker
Northern 3-toed Woodpecker
Eastern Kingbird
Eastern Phoebe
Yellow-bellied Flycatcher
Traill's Flycatcher
Least Flycatcher

Eastern Wood Peewee
Olive-sided Flycatcher
Horned Lark
Tree Swallow
Bank Swallow
Barn Swallow
Cliff Swallow
Gray Jay
Blue Jay
Common Raven
Common Crow
Black-capped Chickadee
Boreal Chickadee
Red-breasted Nuthatch
Brown Creeper
Starling
Solitary Vireo
Red-eyed Vireo
Philadelphia Vireo
Black and White Warbler
Tennessee Warbler
Nashville Warbler
Parula Warbler
Yellow Warbler
Magnolia Warbler
Cape May Warbler
Black-throated Blue Warbler
Myrtle Warbler
Black-throated Green Warbler
Blackburnian Warbler
Chestnut-sided Warbler
Bay-breasted Warbler
Palm Warbler
Ovenbird
Northern Waterthrush
Connecticut Warbler
Mourning Warbler
Yellowthroat
Wilson's Warbler
American Redstart
House Sparrow
Western Meadowlark
Red-winged Blackbird
Baltimore Oriole
Rusty Blackbird
Brewer's Blackbird
Common Grackle

Brown-headed Cowbird
Bonaparte's Gull
Common Tern
Black Tern
Mourning Dove
Rock Dove
Black-billed Cuckoo
Great Horned Owl
Hawk Owl
Barred Owl
Great Gray Owl
Saw-whet Owl
Whip-poor-will
Common Nighthawk
Chimney Swift
Ruby-throated Hummingbird
House Wren
Winter Wren
Long-billed Marsh Wren
Short-billed Marsh Wren
Mockingbird
Catbird
Brown Thrasher
Robin
Hermit Thrush

Swainson's Thrush
Veery
Eastern Bluebird
Golden-crowned Kinglet
Ruby-crowned Kinglet
Cedar Waxwing
Scarlet Tanager
Rose-breasted Grosbeak
Indigo Bunting
Evening Grosbeak
Purple Finch
Pine Siskin
American Goldfinch
Red Crossbill
White-winged Crossbill
Savannah Sparrow
Vesper Sparrow
Slate-coloured Junco
Chipping Sparrow
Clay-coloured Sparrow
White-throated Sparrow
Lincoln's Sparrow
Swamp Sparrow
Song Sparrow